Word for Windows 6
An Active-Learning Approach

Sue Coles

Department of Business and Management Studies,
Crewe and Alsager Faculty, Manchester Metropolitan University

Jenny Rowley

School of Management and Social Sciences,
Edge Hill College of Higher Education

DP Publications Ltd
Aldine Place
London W12 8AW

1995

acknowledgments

This book would not have been completed or even conceived without the support that the authors have received during its production from many of their colleagues and family.

First and foremost we are grateful to the Microsoft Corporation for permission to reproduce various screen dumps and for the creation of a word processing package that is both powerful and fun to work with.

Secondly, teaching Word to our students on the HND in Business Studies and Finance has given us a true insight into the problems that students encounter when learning to use Word. No two people approach a software package with the same knowledge and experience and expectations. We hope that working with our many students we have gained an insight into the use of Word that has informed our approach in this book. We acknowledge a particular debt to Julie Smith whose project provided the inspiration for many of the exercises in this book.

Thirdly, we are ever grateful for the competent and cheerful technical support that has been lent to us by members of the staff of the Computer Services Department in the Crewe and Alsager Faculty. We would like to make special mention of Kate McDonald, Mike Eddleston, and Martin Shenton without whose technical support we would not have been able to find the time or inclination to be able to complete this endeavour.

Lastly, but not least, we are especially grateful for the support of our husbands Martyn and Peter, and our children Helen, Lynsey, Shula and Zeta, during the final phases of the completion of this text, when they had to make do with even less of our time than usual.

A CIP record for this book is available from the British Library.

ISBN 1 85805 121 5

Typeset by Elizabeth Elwin, London

Printed in Great Britain by The Guernsey Press Co Ltd, Vale, Guernsey CI

contents

preface

aims

This book is intended for students on a wide variety of business studies and other courses who need to know how to use MS Word for Windows, one of the industry standard word processing packages. The book assumes no prior experience of other word processing packages.

Although this book is specifically designed for business studies students the orientation will be equally applicable to students in further and higher education on many courses where students need to learn to word process their assignments or projects.

This book is designed for business studies students on a wide range of courses, including BTEC National, BTEC Higher and undergraduate courses in business studies, accountancy, computing and information systems.

approach

This book introduces students to the basics of word processing through a series of applications oriented exercises. The approach is structured to focus on the end-product, whether that product be a letter, memo, advertisement, curriculum vitae, project report, thesis or other document. A series of self contained sessions takes the student through the production of various document types and gradually introduces the student to the features and functions of the word processing package. Each session comprises a series of exercises. As each new function is introduced, the book explains both why the function is useful and how to use it.

The approach is designed not only to introduce students to Word but also to offer them a conceptual framework for word processing that will facilitate the development of transferable skills.

The learning material requires little, if any, input by lecturers, and can therefore be used in programmes based on independent learning. Students learn by practising the commands and techniques to produce specific types of documents.

Word for Windows is a sophisticated package including many desk top publishing type features, graphics and drawing utilities. The text is selective and does not deal will all of these in detail, but does take students step-by-step to a level at which they can happily use the help system or software manual to master further features.

The exercises follow a theme. Many, but not all of the exercises lead towards the creation of a student report. This report is concerned with the development of a new fitness facility in a leisure centre. In order to minimise the amount of keying necessary to complete the exercises, early exercises create documents that are re-used later in the book. By Session 5 various earlier documents will be drawn together to produce a project report. Later sessions deal with specific topics and facilities that may be used to enhance the report further or that may be used in alternative contexts such as in the creation of a newsletter.

In Word there are often many ways of achieving the same operation. This book offers the quickest and most user friendly means of achieving set objectives. Although at times other methods may also be indicated, preference is given to operations based on the use of the mouse and menu options. This approach makes maximum use of the self explanatory nature of the menu options and dialog boxes, and does not ask the user to remember key combinations. Key combinations are indicated against menu options in the system, and the user may familiarise themselves with these as their experience in using the software develops.

How to use this book

Students who have not used a Windows program before should first read through Appendix 1 **Basic Windows Operations** (page 149), which summarises the key features of the Windows environment, and then turn to **An overview of Word for Windows** (page viii) before tackling Session 1. Students who are familiar with the Windows environment should also read through **An overview of Word for Windows** before beginning Session 1.

Students can refer to Appendix 2 **Buttons on the default toolbar** (page 153) whenever they need reminding of the functions of each button on the toolbars. Appendix 3 **Customising Word** (page 155) is intended for:

a) those whose Word system has been customised so that it does not use the default settings assumed in this book (students should ask lecturers to perform the necessary commands to return their system to its default setting);

b) those students who, having worked through all the sessions in the book, feel confident enough to create their own settings for Word.

Conventions

The following conventions have been adopted to distinguish between the various objects on the screen:

- Commands are shown in bold and italic e.g. *File-Page Setup*, which means choose the *File* menu and then select the option *Page Setup* from that menu.
- Buttons and Icons are shown in bold e.g. **Cancel**
- Dialog box names are shown in bold e.g. **Border Paragraphs**
- Keys are shown in bold and caps e.g. **CTRL**
- Filenames are shown in bold e.g. **Termref**

An overview of Word for Windows

All students (except those who have some experience of Word for Windows) should read this section before tackling Session 1 (page 1). Appendix 1 reviews the basic features of Windows for the benefit of inexperienced users or as a ready reference for those who may have forgotten some of the basic features. Appendix 1 also introduces mouse techniques and acts as a summary of the terminology used elsewhere in this book.

a tour of the Word for Windows screen

It is worthwhile to study the Word for Windows screen for a few moments before trying to make use of it. There is rather a lot of information summarised in the next two pages. A quick read should serve to orientate you, but do not expect to remember all of this detail. This section can be used as a ready reference and returned to as necessary.

The Word screen can be formatted in a number of different ways. to make sure that you are looking at the same screen as described in this text, choose **View** and switch on a tick against **Ruler**. From the **View** menu click on **Toolbars** and check that there is an x by the Standard and Formatting toolbars.

Now choose **Tools-Options**, then **View**, and make sure that there are crosses against **Horizontal Scroll Bar**, and **Status Bar**.

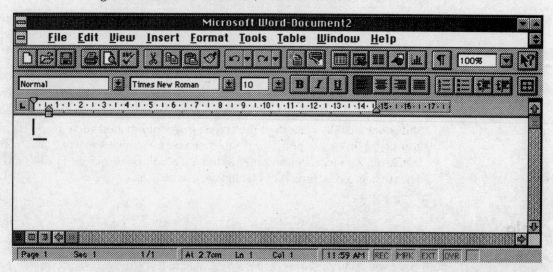

The Word screen that you should now be viewing has the following components:

1. **Title bar** – shows the name of the document (or Document X if you have yet to name the document).

2. **Word control menu** – in the very top left hand corner. If you click on this box a menu with commands for sizing and moving the Word window, switching to other applications and closing Word, is displayed.

3. **Document control menu** – in the top left hand corner, but below the Word control menu. If you click on this box a menu with commands for sizing, moving, splitting and closing documents, and for moving the insertion point between windows is displayed.

4. **Word main menu** – shows the main pull down menus, such as *File, Edit, View, Insert, Format, Tools, Table, Window* and *Help*.

5. **Standard Toolbar** – shows a series of icons which can be used to perform some commands quickly. The actions of the buttons are listed in Appendix 2. If you point to a button for several seconds a small box appears showing the name of the button which gives an idea of its function.

6. **Formatting Toolbar** – shows the character and paragraph formatting in force at the current position of the insertion point. It displays character formatting such as font, size, and whether it is bold, italics and so on, and paragraph formatting such as left or right justification. On the left of this toolbar are the font and point size boxes. To the right are a series of buttons. The meaning of these buttons is shown in appendix 2.

   The font and point size can be changed by clicking on the down arrow by one of these boxes, viewing the alternatives, and clicking on one of the options. The icons on the right both show the current state of the text and allow it to be changed. For example, to change characters to italic it is necessary to select the characters and click the italic button. The italic button goes in and stays in whilst the cursor is moving over italic characters.

   On the left of the toolbar is the style box, which indicates the style that has been used to format the selection. Styles allow you to format your document more easily.

7. **Ruler** – gives information about the indentation and tab stops of the selected paragraph. Indents appear as tiny triangles, tabs as shapes indicating their function.

8. **Status bar** – at the bottom of the screen gives information such as the location of the insertion point, and whether you have switches such as **CAPS LOCK** on. At various times other information will be displayed in the status bar, such as a description of highlighted commands.

help

Both help and examples and demos are available for Word for Windows. There are four main methods of getting into the help system:

1. Pull down the *Help* menu and select a command from it.

2. At any time you can press the **F1** key to get help on whatever you are doing at that moment.

3. In many dialog boxes there is a **HELP** button

4. Press **SHIFT+F1**. The pointer changes with a question mark after it and it can be used to point to anything. Clicking on that object will then bring up help. For instance, in this way you may get help on the meaning of all of the items in the status bar.

examples and demos

The examples and demos are useful for introducing a range of basic topics. They can be accessed by choosing *Help-Examples and demos*.

exercise 0.1

This exercise encourages you to explore the help system and to start to use the Word window.

Click on the *Help* menu on the Word main menu. This should cause the pull down menu to be displayed. Click on *Help Index* to open the **Help Index** window. View the contents of this window. When you have finished close this window by clicking on the Control menu in the upper left hand corner of the window (if you are not sure where this is consult Appendix 1), and click on the Close option to close the window.

If you would like to examine the tutorials, click on *Help* on the Word main menu again, and choose *Learning Word*.

ten basic tips

Use these tips to refer to if you get stuck as you work through the exercises in the sessions that follow.

1. Always Select, then Do. For example, when you want to change text, first select it and then choose a command or click on a button that will do what you want.

2. Save your document regularly, say every 15-20 minutes. The fastest way to save is to click on the Save button on the standard toolbar.

3. If you do not like what you have just done, undo it using *Edit-Undo* or by clicking on the **Undo** button in the toolbar. Word6 will allow you to undo more than one operation.

4. **F1** accesses on-line Help.

5. Do not press **ENTER** at the end of every line. Only press **ENTER** at the end of a paragraph.

6. Do make full use of the table feature to create tables.

7. Do not use the **SPACEBAR** to create indents. Set indents by using the ruler, or *Format-Paragraph*, or the **Indent** button on the formatting toolbar.

8. Use the standard toolbar to complete most common tasks.

9. Use the formatting toolbar to apply formatting to your document.

10. Use the ruler to adjust margins, tab settings and table columns.

Session 1
Basics

objectives

In this session basic operations that are fundamental to the effective use of Word are introduced. At the end of this session you will be able to:

- enter Word for Windows
- create a simple document
- save a document
- close a document
- exit Word for Windows
- open a document
- edit a document
- print a document

Such operations will allow you to construct simple letters and memos.

The simple documents created in this session can be further improved by the use of other facilities described later in this text.

The operations covered in this session are essential to the successful creation of any document. For example, it is essential to be confident that you have saved a document before going on to create longer or more sophisticated documents.

Once you are familiar with Word for Windows, you will perform most of the operations covered in this Session again and again. The sequence adopted in this Session is significant. Always remember to save a document after you have created it and before performing other operations, such as printing.

When you have completed this Session you will have grasped some important basics. Word for Windows has a number of default settings, such as A4 paper size, and specified margins which you may wish to adjust later in order to change the document's appearance, but for this Session you should accept the default settings. These default settings usually allow you to create your first documents very painlessly.

activity 1.1 Creating a simple new document

This activity takes you into Word for Windows, asks you to open a new document, to type in a simple letter and to make corrections.

Entering Word for Windows

Microsoft
Word

To enter Word for Windows double click on the Word for Windows icon in your Windows program group. Whilst the software is loading the pointer will be displayed as an egg timer. Word for Windows will open with a new document ready for you to enter text. A Tip of the Day may be displayed and you may read this and other tips before clicking on **OK**. The screen should show the basic Word screen (as in the Overview), with an empty document automatically open for you.

Entering Text

Text can be entered via the keyboard. The only important difference between word processing and typing at this stage is that you should not press the **ENTER** key at the end of a line. Instead, if you continue typing, the text wraps automatically onto the new line. If you do press the **ENTER** key this will prevent the effective formatting of documents later. **ENTER** should only be pressed when you wish to commence a new paragraph, or to execute a command.

Making running corrections

Simple corrections of one to two characters or words can be made by placing the insertion point by the character to be amended.

The insertion point can be positioned by:

❐ position the mouse pointer where you want the insertion point to be and click.

or

❐ Pressing the **ARROW** keys.

Remember that you cannot position the insertion point past the end mark at the end of a document.

Next apply whichever of the following is appropriate:

❐ the **BACKSPACE** key – to delete characters to the left of the cursor

❐ the **DEL** key – to delete characters to the right of the cursor

❐ key in additional characters

exercise 1.1

This exercise creates a simple letter.

❐ Enter Word for Windows.

❐ Type in the simple letter below.

❐ Make any necessary running corrections.

❐ Do not forget that you should *not* press **ENTER** at the end of each line unless a new paragraph is required.

❏ Once you have created the letter move on to Activity 1.2 which asks you to save the letter for later use.

Chelmer Leisure and Recreation Centre
Park View Road
Chelmer
Cheshire
CE9 1JS

Universal Gym (Europe) Ltd
Hutton
Brentwood
Essex
CM13 1XA

17 October 1994

Dear Sir

Health and Fitness Centre for Chelmer Leisure and Recreation Centre

As part of my studies for my BA in Business Studies, Sport and Recreation, I am conducting a project on behalf of Chelmer Leisure and Recreation Centre.

Chelmer Leisure and Recreation Centre wishes to investigate the options for the enhancement of their health and fitness facilities. Currently I am approaching a number of potential suppliers with a view to collecting information on the range of equipment available in the marketplace. I would therefore be grateful if you would supply me with appropriate publicity literature and equipment specifications, together with price lists.

Thank you

Yours faithfully

Ms S Leveridge.

---

activity 1.2 Saving documents and exiting Word for Windows

This activity introduces you to saving documents, closing documents and exiting Word for Windows.

Saving a document

 To save a document use *File-Save* or click on the **SAVE** icon on the toolbar. The first time a new document is being saved this will bring the **Save As** dialog box onto the screen. This contains the following boxes:

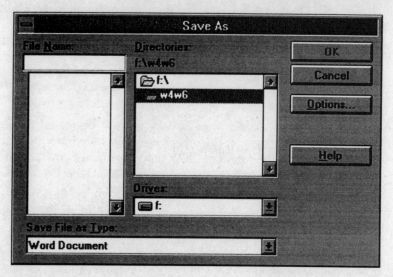

File Name This shows the names of the files in the current directory, these names being any other documents that you may have created and provides a box for you to type a filename. In default mode the documents displayed are all word processor created documents.

Directories This shows the directories available to you within your current drive.

Drive This shows the drives available to you. The range of these will depend on whether your system is stand alone or networked, the system configuration and any security arrangements. For example, for a stand alone system the normal drive for the hard disc is C:

Save File as Type This shows the different types of file formats which you may choose to save your file as. For example, you might wish to save the document in a format used by another word processor e.g. Word for Windows 2.0, WordPerfect or simply in a text form i.e. Text Only.

For your first document it should be sufficient to enter the filename in the box at the top of the **File Name** box, and click on **OK** or press **ENTER**. When you save a document for the first time, Word may display the **Summary Information** dialog box. By default Word does not display this and the only effect you should observe is that the name you have given to your document appears in the title bar. The Summary Information can be used to enter important details of a document that may help its recall later. See Appendix 3 for changing the Summary Information dialog display option.

Once you have saved a document it may be saved on subsequent occasions by using *File-Save*.

It is good practice to save a long document every twenty minutes or so. Certainly make sure to save every document before attempting to print it. Word offers an autosaving function which is described in Appendix 3.

More on Filenames

File names for Word documents may be from one to eight characters in length, followed by, optionally, a period and a one to three character filename extension. Any characters may be used except spaces and the following characters: * ? , ; [ ] + = \ / : < >. You cannot use a period except to separate the filename from the extension.

Filename extensions are usually used to distinguish between different types of files. For example, document files generally have the extension .DOC, backup files have the extension .BAK, and if you have any spreadsheet files created with Excel these will have the extension .XLS. Generally, there is no need to type the extension as Word automatically adds .DOC.

Choose meaningful filenames so that you can easily retrieve your documents later. For instance the letter in Exercise 1.2 could be saved using the name of the recipient, e.g. **UniGym 1.DOC**, to make it easier to recall.

If you wish to save more than one version of a document, you may save the later version of the document under a different filename, as discussed below.

Closing documents

Once you have finished working on a document, and have saved it you may wish to close it. Closing a document is the equivalent of putting the document away in a manual system. All documents must be closed before exiting Word for Windows. If you try to exit with unsaved documents open, Word for Windows will ask you if you wish to save and close documents. In a Windows application such as Word for Windows you may have a number of document windows open at any one time. It is not necessary to close one document before opening a different or new document in a different window. But, new Windows users should be wary of opening too many documents at once. It is easy to convince yourself that you have lost your work when it is merely on a hidden window. So, to start with, close all documents as you finish with them. Documents can be closed by *File-Close* or by double clicking on the document Control menu box in the upper left corner of the document window. When you have closed all documents the application background appears and the menu bar changes so that only *File* and *Help* appear on the **Menu Bar**.

Exiting from Word for Windows

When you wish to leave Word for Windows, choose *File-Exit*. Alternatively, you may double click on the **Control menu** box at the top left of the screen and select *Close*, or use the keyboard shortcut **ALT-F4**.

exercise 1.2

To save the document that you created in Exercise 1.1 as **Letter1:**

❏ click on *File-Save.*

❏ enter **Letter1** in the **filename** box.

☐ click on **OK**

☐ Close the document, using ***File-Close***.

☐ Exit from Word for Windows, by clicking on ***File-Exit***.

activity 1.3 Opening and editing a document

This activity takes you back into Word for Windows, asks you to open an existing document, to make appropriate amendments and to save the amended document under a different filename.

Opening a document

To open an existing document use ***File-Open*** or click on the document icon on the Toolbar. This causes the **Open** dialogue box to be displayed. The **Open** dialog box has a similar layout to the Save As dialog box. Click on an appropriate filename and click on **OK**, or alternatively double click on the filename. If there are more files than can be displayed in the box, either click on the down arrow or drag the scroll box to view the other filenames.

Insert and Overwrite

Normally you use the word processor in insert mode, that is, the existing text will be moved up to make room for any new text. By pressing the **INS** (Insert) key you can change to the overwrite mode which will allow you to type over existing text. To return to insert mode press the **INS** key again. Note that the letters **OVR** in the status bar appear black when you are in overwrite mode and grey in insert mode.

Saving another copy

An additional copy of a document can be saved simply by choosing ***File-Save As*** and entering a new file name. This will create two copies of the document under different names. Alternatively, two copies may be stored under the same name, but in different drives or directories. For example, you may wish to save an additional copy on a directory on the A: drive so that one copy is saved to floppy disk. To switch to a different directory, in the **Save As** dialog box, click on it with the mouse and click **OK**, or just double click on it to perform both selecting and opening the directory at the same time. Drives can be changed similarly using the Drives list.

exercise 1.3

This exercise creates a second updated version of the document **Letter1** whilst keeping the first version.

☐ Re-enter Word for Windows.

☐ Open the document called **Letter1**.

❑ Add the following paragraph at the end of the text of the letter, before 'Thank you'.

> I shall contact you again within a few weeks for more detailed discussions if the Leisure and Recreation Centre Manager feels that your equipment might meet our requirements.

❑ Save the new file using *File-Save As*, but this time using the file name **Letter2**.

❑ You should now have two files, called **Letter1**, and **Letter2**, respectively. Inspect the **File Name** box to check that this is the case.

❑ Click on **OK** to return to close the dialog box.

activity 1.4 Printing a document

You will normally print a document when it is open and being displayed on your screen. You should always view your document in Print Preview before printing, in order to check the general layout of the page. The quickest way to create a printed copy is to issue the *File-Print Preview* command (or click on the Print Preview button), and then, once in Print Preview, click on the **PRINT** button.

Using *File-Print* from either the document view or the print preview will bring up the **Print** dialog box. Usually you can safely accept all of the default settings, so just click on **OK**, and provided that your printer is on, loaded with paper and on-line, printing should commence.

This is a very simple approach to printing. Below we briefly review the options available in printing. There are a number of parameters that can be set. You may wish to skip these for now and return to them later. These parameters are set under the *Print Preview*, *Page Setup*, *Page Layout* and *Print Setup* options. These are outlined below.

Print Preview Screen

All documents should be viewed either using *Print Preview* on the *File* menu, or the *Page Layout* command on the *View* menu, before being printed.

The **Print Preview** screen has the following buttons in its toolbar:

PRINT clicking the Print button on the toolbar will print one copy of a document quickly using the current print settings.

ZOOM allows you to zoom-in and zoom-out

ONE PAGE displays only one page at a time of the document. Use Page Up or Page Down keys to move through the pages of your document.

MULTIPLE PAGE allows you to switch between the display of two or more pages on the screen.

ZOOM CONTROL controls how large or small a document appears on the screen. You can enlarge the display to make it easier to read or reduce the display to view an entire page.

VIEW RULER displays vertical and horizontal rulers for adjusting the top, bottom, left and right margins. These can be adjusted by dragging the markers on the rulers.

SHRINK TO FIT if only a few lines of your document appear on the last page you may be able to reduce the number of pages using this option.

HIDE click on this button to only display the previewed page(s) and the Print Preview toolbar. To display all elements click on this button again.

CLOSE closes the Print Preview screen and returns you to your document view.

HELP click on this to create a Help pointer. Click the Help pointer on any item on the screen to display help information.

Print Dialog Box

The Print dialog box is displayed when the ***File-Print*** command is used. It allows a number of options to be set. These include:

❑ Printer – the current printer is shown

❑ Print What- shows the document type

❑ Copies – shows the number of copies to be printed

❑ Range – shows which sections of the document are to be printed either, all, current page, selection (if one is made), or specified pages.

❑ Print – this drop-down list allows the choice between all pages, odd pages or even pages to be made. If you wish to print double-sided then this can be achieved by printing all the odd pages, putting the paper back in the printer, reversed, and printing all the even pages.

❑ The **PRINTER** button – if you have more than one printer available then clicking on this displays the Printer Setup dialog box, from which you can select the desired printer.

❑ The **OPTIONS** button – takes you to the Options dialog box. The Options dialog box offers a range of more specialised printing options such as draft output, reverse print order or print hidden text.

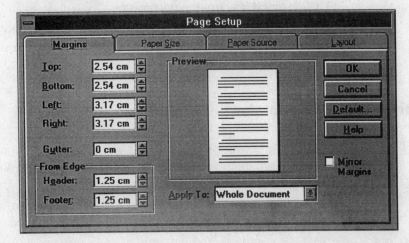

Page Setup

Page Setup, on the *File* menu, allows you to set a number of parameters which specify how the document will be displayed on the page. Four main options are available:

❏ Margins

❏ Paper Size

❏ Paper Source

❏ Layout

and each of these has a separate dialog box which are arranged like a series of index cards. The required dialog box is displayed when the appropriate 'index card label' is clicked on. Many of the options in these dialog boxes are self-explanatory and the preview helps to indicate the effect of modifications.

In Margins, two important characteristics are:

❏ the part of the document to which the settings are to be applied

❏ whether facing pages need to be set with different margins, as in a book, to allow for binding.

Print Setup

If you always use the same printer with the same size paper and with other standard settings you may rarely need to use Print Setup. However, **Print Setup** does offer considerable flexibility for choosing various printing parameters.

Choose *File-Print* and click on the **Printer** button. This displays the **Print Setup** dialog box. Here all of the printers available to you will be displayed. Choose the one that you want to use, and then click on **OK**.

If you click on the **OPTIONS** button a dialog box allowing further options such as intensity control will be displayed.

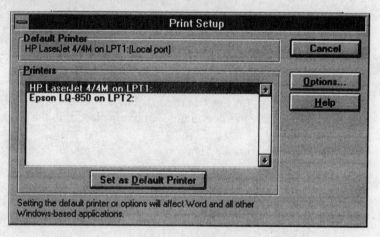

exercise 1.4

This exercise asks you to print the document **Letter2**.

❏ With the document called **Letter2** displayed on the screen choose *File-Print Preview* to view the document in **Print Preview**.

❏ Click on the **PRINT** button to call up the **Print** dialog box.

❏ Click on **OK** to print the document.

Could you print this document in landscape? Try to set this up using *File-Page Setup* and selecting the Layout option. View the result on screen with **Print Preview**.

activity 1.5 Document views

Prior to printing your document you will have viewed your document in print preview. Word offers several different ways of looking at your document, each of which is suitable for a different purpose. These are:

Normal View is the default view. Text formatting is shown, such as line spacing, font and point size, but the layout of the page is simplified.

Outline View helps you to examine the logical structure of your document. You can choose to display just the headings. To reorganise a document you can simply drag a heading to another place in the outline, and all associated text moves with the heading. You can also raise or lower a heading's level of importance in the outline.

Page Layout View shows you how each page of your document will look when printed. You can edit and format the text and see the result on the screen.

Master Document is used when very long documents are created which are better stored in several files rather than one file. A master document allows you to work with all the files so the document appears to be one. Master document view is similar to Outline view.

Print Preview is similar to Page Layout View, but displays whole pages at a reduced size and allows you to adjust various aspects of page layout, but not to edit the text.

You will probably use Normal View and Page Layout View most often. Normal View is useful whilst you get your text typed and corrected, and then, Page Layout can be used to adjust the formatting and layout.

Using the ***Zoom*** command on the ***View*** menu, or the list box on the toolbar, you can reduce or magnify the display size of a document from 25 percent to 200 percent. The magnification or reduction affects only the screen display.

exercise 1.5

With the document called **Letter2** on the screen, experiment with different document views, first by selecting different views from the ***View*** menu, and then by selecting ***Print Preview*** from the ***File*** menu.

activity 1.6 Edit-Undo

The ***Edit-Undo*** command is a valuable fail-safe. Any time that you issue a command or type or delete some text, you can Undo this by issuing the ***Edit-Undo*** command. This is very useful for retrieving mistakes, and moving back to a previous state. Word maintains a history of the commands you have given it and it is possible to undo a command that was not your last command.

exercise 1.6

In the document **Letter2**, change 'Yours faithfully' to 'Yours sincerely'. Then use ***Edit-Undo*** to undo the change. Try changing other words in the text of the document, and then undoing the changes.

exercise 1.7

In the document **Letter2**, change 'Yours faithfully' to 'Yours sincerely'. Next change the date to today's date. To undo both of these two changes:

❏ Open the Undo list box.

❏ Select the last 2 actions by dragging, or by pressing the down arrow key once and pressing **ENTER**.

Session 2
Formatting Text

objectives

At the end of this session you will be able to use the following types of text formatting:

- [ ] typefonts: these are the forms of type i.e. bold, italics, underlining, condensed type and also the size of the letters.

- [ ] typefaces: these are the design of the type and have names such as Times New Roman, Courier etc.

- [ ] justification: this is the way in which the text is aligned between the margins.

- [ ] margins

- [ ] line spacing

Such formatting will allow you to construct simple:

- [ ] advertisements

- [ ] posters or other display documents

These can be further improved by the use of other facilities described later in this text. For example, you may wish to add graphics or a border to any of these documents.

Formatting is used to make the text look appealing to the reader and is used to draw attention to headings or important points within the document.

With a powerful word processor such as Word6 for Windows you have at your disposal many choices of typeface and typefont. Some typefaces are available in many different sizes. This is another way, in addition to the use of bold, italic and underlined type, in which to highlight or emphasise parts of your document.

Other forms of formatting you may apply are adjustment of the margins, justification and line spacing.

Quite often it is easier to key in text without any formatting and concentrate on the content of the work. Later formatting and proof reading may be accomplished as a combined task. Alternatively formatting may be applied at the time of keying, especially if the document is short such as an advertisement or report cover.

activity 2.1 Selecting Text

Text must be selected before its format can be changed. Text selection is also used to mark a piece of text for deletion, copying or other operations. Most of the operations described in this and later sessions require text to be selected first.

Don't forget that the word processor will not change anything if you do not select the part of the document you wish to reformat first.

Any area of selected text will be highlighted. The colour of the highlight depends upon the Windows colour setting used. If the Windows default colour setting is used then the highlight is black. The various methods of selecting parts of a document are summarised in the table below:

Selection using the mouse

word	move the mouse cursor to the word you wish to select and double-click on the left mouse button.
line	move the mouse cursor into the left hand edge of the screen (the pointer changes to a right-pointing white arrow) level with the line you wish to select and click the left button.
paragraph	move the mouse cursor into the left hand edge level with the paragraph you wish to select and double-click the left button.
whole document	move the mouse cursor into the left hand edge, press the **CTRL** key and click the left hand mouse button.
section of your choice	move the mouse cursor to the beginning of the section, click the left mouse button and holding it down drag the cursor to the end of the section. If you start your selection in the middle of a word and end it in the middle of another word the selection will automatically adjust to include the whole of the first and last word.
undoing a selection	move the mouse pointer to anywhere in the document and click the left button.
adjusting a selection	hold down the **SHIFT** key and click at the point where you wish the selection to end. **Note**: if you initially selected whole units of text e.g. lines or paragraphs then the selection will expand or contract by these units, otherwise it will expand or contract by whole words.

Selection using the keyboard

Move the insertion point to the place in your document where you wish the selection to begin, hold down the **SHIFT** key and use the direction **ARROW** keys to move the insertion point to the end of your selection.

To adjust the selection, hold down the **SHIFT** key and using the direction **ARROW** keys expand or contract your selection. To cancel your selection press an **ARROW** key without holding down the **SHIFT** key.

exercise 2.1

Key in the following text, which is the terms of reference for a report and save it as **Termref.**

Terms of reference

This feasibility study looks at a complete refurbishment of the multigym at Chelmer Leisure and Recreation Centre. A wide variety of equipment could be offered in a modern fitness suite. This equipment would be a vast improvement on the existing equipment. Various equipment manufacturers have been approached and three have submitted proposals for refurbishment. This report considers each of the proposals received.

The companies from which proposals have been received are:-

UNIVERSAL GYM (EUROPE) LTD
ATLANTA SPORTS INDUSTRIES LTD
PHYSIQUE TRAINING EQUIPMENT LTD

Each proposal consists of a list of equipment and plans for the fitness room, plus costings. The proposals are detailed and analysed in the report. The result of the analysis of the proposals will be a recommendation for the best option.

The report will then consider how a new fitness suite would affect the centre's usage. It will also consider ways in which the new facility should be marketed.

Make the following selections and after each selection undo it.

❒ Select the word 'feasibility'.

❒ Select the first line in the first paragraph.

❒ Select the last paragraph.

❒ Select the whole document.

❒ Select 'Chelmer Leisure and Recreation Centre'.

Remember that when you have made a successful selection, the selection will be highlighted.

Experiment with selecting words, lines, paragraphs, the whole document, and sections of your choice. You need to move on to the next and subsequent sections to make use of these selections.

activity 2.2 Using typefonts

A character may be printed in **bold** or *italic* type or <u>underlined</u>. Bold type or underlining are often used for headings so as to distinguish them from the rest of the text. Typefaces are also used to put emphasis on to a section of text.

Selection of typefonts – using the mouse

As you type you can change the typefont as you go along by simply depressing the required button(s) in the **Formatting** tool bar:

To depress a button simply move the mouse pointer to it and click and any subsequent typing will take the typefont you have set. To 'switch off' the typefont simply depress the button again. When a button is depressed it appears a lighter grey than the surrounding area.

To choose from the different underlining options:

❒ Use the *Format-Font* command.

❒ In the **Font** dialog box, with the Font 'tab' selected, open the Underline list box, by clicking on its associated down arrow.

❒ Select the type of underlining required, this can be none, single, words only, double or dotted.

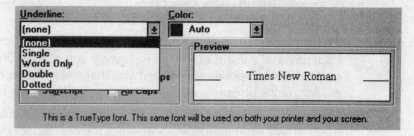

❒ click on **OK.**

More than one typefont may be used at once, for example ***bold italic double underlined*** or **bold, dotted underlined** text.

Selection of typefonts – using the keyboard

Formatting may be applied using the keyboard instead of the mouse using the following key combinations.

Typefont	CTRL+
Bold	B
Italic	I
Underline	U

Typefont	CTRL+SHIFT+
Word underline	W
Double underline	D

To reformat existing text, first select the text you wish to re-format and then choose the appropriate mouse or keyboard actions.

exercise 2.2

Open the document **Termref** created in the previous exercise. Select the heading and make it bold and underlined. Embold the name of the leisure centre and put the company names in italics. Save the document. Experiment by making your own selections and changing their typefont, but do not save these changes.

exercise 2.3

Start a new document and type in the following memo. Select the required typefont i.e. bold, italics and underline before keying in the text. Save as **Appmemo**.

---

the ***MANCHESTER METROPOLITAN UNIVERSITY***

Crewe + Alsager Faculty

MEMORANDUM

TO: R. S. Symmond

FROM: Peter Jackson

Date: 12th Feb. 9X

Subject: <u>Final year business project</u>

When I saw you last, you suggested three possible times when we could discuss my project work. I would like to confirm that the first, *2:00pm on Monday 16th*, would suit me best and I shall see you then unless you let me know otherwise.

---

activity 2.3 Fonts

What is a font? Word uses the word **font** to describe a typeface and it's size. The typeface is the design or shape of a set of characters. Most modern printers have standard fonts such as Times Roman, Helvetica, and Courier included in the printer's hardware. These are known as **printer fonts**. It is also possible to obtain soft fonts, i.e. printer fonts that are downloaded to the printer from the computer.

Word for Windows allows you to see on screen exactly what will be printed out. This is known as WYSIWYG a mnemonic for '*What you see is what you get*'. In order to do this, Word uses screen representations of the printer fonts. Screen fonts usually match printer fonts closely. If the font Courier 5cpi, a printer font is chosen, Word will display the text in a manner which does represent the spacing.

Some of the fonts provided with the printer have fixed spacing. This means that each character is the same width as every other character. Typefaces such as Courier are designed like this, so that they can be used with simple word processing packages that have no capacity for complex formatting. More sophisticated packages, such as Word, can take advantage of **proportionally spaced** fonts. With these, naturally wider characters, such as the letter *m*, are given more space than narrower ones, such as *j*.

A fixed space font A proportionally spaced font

Courier Times Roman

The font that you are using will appear in the font list box in the toolbar. If you are using the standard default font it will have **Times New Roman** in it. On the right of this list box there is another which contains a number; this is the point size of the characters. If you are using the default font then it will have the number **10** in it.

Choosing different fonts

Choice of font is a matter of personal taste which should be tempered by consideration for the type of document being produced.

Having chosen a particular font it is usual to use it throughout the main body of the document. Different sizes of the chosen typeface can be used for titles, headings, headers and footers. A different font from normal could be used as an alternative to draw attention to a particular portion of the text.

The font list box in the toolbar can be opened by clicking on the down arrow box to the right. The box expands to show a list of the different fonts that are available. Printer fonts have a small printer symbol next to them. Some fonts have two T's next to them (see illustration following), these are known as true type fonts and they are the most versatile of the screen fonts because they can be varied in size in steps of one point.

To select a font and a size for that font:

❏ Open the **Font** list box.

❏ Use the scroll bar to move through the list. There are more fonts than can be displayed in the box. The list of fonts available to you will depend upon the type of printer you have installed.

❏ Click on the name of your chosen font.

❏ Open the **Point Size** list box.

❏ Use the scroll bar to move through the list of sizes. Different fonts will have different sets of sizes available.

❑ Click on the size required.

The font called Symbol uses the letters of the Greek alphabet; this can be useful if you are writing a scientific report. Also there is a true type font called Wingdings which gives a variety of shapes and symbols, such as:

exercise 2.4

Using **Termref** created in Exercise 2.1, select each company name one at a time and apply a different font. Apply different fonts to each paragraph. Note that this creates a document that is unpleasing to read, but is a useful means of exploring the fonts available to you.

exercise 2.5

Type in the text outlined below:

> Questions of feasibility
> Technical feasibility
> Is the equipment available to support the project?
> Operational feasibility
> Will staff changes or training be necessary?
> Economic feasibility
> Will the benefits from the project outweigh the costs?

The first 3 lines are written using various sizes of the true type font **Arial**. The next two lines are **Times New Roman**. The last two lines are **Courier**. Do not save this.

activity 2.4 Controlling margins

There are three margins which you can control and these are:

❑ the left margin is the position of the left edge of the text.

❑ the right margin is the position of the right edge of the text.

❑ the indent margin is the position of the left edge of the **first line** of a paragraph.

The positions of the edges of the text on the page can be adjusted using *File-Page Setup*. In the **Page Setup** dialog box the settings can be viewed and adjusted. There are default settings for the position of the edge of the text. For example, the default setting of the edge of the text for A4 paper is 3.17cm in from the sides. The position of the text in relation to the top and bottom of the paper may also be adjusted.

By default the left and right margins will be at the edges of the text as defined in Page Setup. The indent margin is at the same position as the left margin.

Adjusting the margins using the ruler

The ruler is displayed below the formatting toolbar and is marked in centimetres (it can be altered to display inches). On the ruler there are three triangular sliders indicating the positions of the left, indent, and the right margins.

The left and right margin sliders are on the bottom of the ruler and the indent margin slider is on the top of the ruler.

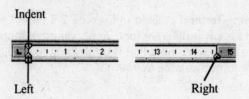

Indent

Left   Right

To change

Left or indent margin	Drag the appropriate margin slider to the required position on the ruler.
Right margin	Drag the right triangle to the required position on the ruler.

Setting Indents

Normal Indent	Drag the indent margin so that it is to the **right** of the left margin.
Hanging Indent	Drag the indent margin so it is to the **left** of the left margin.

Any adjustment made to the margins will affect the document at the current insertion point position and any text keyed in thereafter. Margin positions may be revised by selected the text needing revision and re-positioning the margin markers.

exercise 2.6

With a new document open, set the left margin to 1cm and the right margin to 13cm. Type in the first paragraph of the text following this paragraph. Set the left margin to 2cm, the indent margin to 3cm and the right margin to 12cm before keying in the second paragraph. The margins for the third paragraph are at left and indent 3cm, right 10cm.

Questionnaires provide a structured and formal way in which information may be collected.

The advantages of questionnaires are that they are relatively inexpensive, they are free from interviewer distortion and if the response is anonymous, personal or controversial questions may be asked.

The disadvantages of questionnaires are that there may be a low response, questions usually have to be simple and straightforward and if they are anonymous then there is no information about the person who has answered them.

Save this document as **Qdesign**.

Changing existing margins

The margins of existing text can be altered by selecting that text and then adjusting the margin positions. If you alter the position of the margins when no text is selected then your alterations will only affect the paragraph that the insertion point is currently in.

Adjusting the margins using the menu

The margins may be altered using *Format-Paragraph*. In the **Paragraph** dialog box, with the Indents and Spacing 'tab' selected, alter the values shown in the **Indentation** section.

In this section there are three boxes, **Left**, **Right** and **Special**. The number in each associated box may be altered to position the margins. The **Special** list box allows the type of indenting to be chosen.

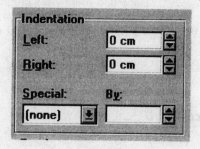

exercise 2.7

Recall **Termref** and change the position of the left margin of the three company name paragraphs.

❏ Select all three paragraphs and drag the left and then the indent margin right by 2cm.

❏ Select the first paragraph and drag the indent margin right by 1cm. Save the document.

Experiment by selecting other portions of the document and altering the left, right and indent margins, but do not save these changes.

Adjusting the left margin using the buttons

Word6 provides a quick way to adjust the left margin by means of two buttons on the tool bar.

The button on the right moves the left margin in to the right by half an inch (1.27cm) and the button on the left moves the left margin out to the left by half an inch.

Hanging Indent

This is where the left and indent margins are set up so that the left margin is to the right of the indent margin. Hanging indents are commonly used where a list of points is being made and the first words of a paragraph need to stand out. As shown in the following example.

CHELMER LEISURE AND RECREATION CENTRE

AEROBICS OPEN DAY

Step   One of the best ways to start your fitness programme. Our fitness demonstrators will be on hand to advise you on a suitable fitness programme.

Cycle   Tone up those flabby thighs and strengthen those backs. Our cycles simulate real cycling conditions which can be individually tailored to your fitness programme.

Row   Fancy yourself in the boat race? Try your hand at our computer controlled rowing machine.

---

exercise 2.8

To create the example above:

❏ Use a new document and type in the two lines of the heading (try to repro-duce the font) and press **ENTER**.

❏ Drag the left margin to the right 4cm.

❏ Key in the type of activity using the font Arial, bold and size 14.

❏ After keying in the activity name press the **TAB** key to 'tab' the insertion point to line up with the left margin.

❏ Enter the rest of the text comprising the activity; it will word wrap around onto the left margin. Use a different typeface such as Courier New, font size 10.

❏ Press **ENTER** for a new line.

❏ Repeat the last 4 steps for each aerobic activity.

❏ Save this document as **Openday**.

Bullets and numbering points

To distinguish a list of points from the rest of the text it is usual to highlight them using bullets or point numbers. A bullet is a symbol at the start of each point as in the following illustration.

FINDINGS FROM MARKET RESEARCH

Information has been collated from the returned questionnaires resulting in:

❏ *a consensus of opinion that present facilities are inadequate and that attendance is poor*

❏ *the numbers of users, particularly female, would increase if the facility was refurbished*

❏ *the majority of users are car owners, so promotion in a wider area could attract new clients*

❏ *nearly two thirds of the people surveyed had never used the existing multigym*

❏ *aerobic activities were popular*

❏ *entertainment, such as satellite television, would be an attraction in the new fitness suite*

Hanging indents, as described above, are used when the text comprises a set of points. Word6 offers two buttons on the toolbar which will help you to type a numbered or bulleted list; these are shown opposite.

By clicking on the numbering button, if it is the first point in a list then **1.** appears with the insertion point ready tabbed onto the left margin. The margins are pre-set so as to create a hanging indent. Each time you press **ENTER** the number of the point will increase by one. A bulleted list can be created in a similar manner using the bullet button. When you have finished the list click on the numbering or bulleting button to 'turn-off' this function.

Bulleting or numbering can be applied after the text has been keyed in as normal paragraphs. When the document is finished re-visit the list, position the insertion point at the beginning of each point in turn and click on the numbering or bulleting icon.

If more than one numbered list is used in a document the numbering may be controlled using *Format-Bullets and Numbering*.

exercise 2.9

> **Five Fab Top Tips to Reduce Fat in Your Diet.**
> 1. Fry less often. Grill, bake, nuke in the microwave or boil instead.
> 2. Trim visible fat off meat, don't eat the skin on chicken, skim fat off casseroles and buy lean cuts.
> 3. Cut down on chocolate, cakes, pastries and biscuits.
> 4. Use less cooking oil or fat, less salad oil, less mayonnaise and other sauces.
> 5. Be aware of the high fat content of some foods perceived as "healthy" such as peanuts, avocado, polyunsaturated margarine and oils and "low fat" spreads.

To create the example above:

- ❏ Start a new document and key in the heading line and create a new line using **ENTER**.

- ❏ Click on the point numbering icon. A number appears and the insertion point will be positioned on the left margin. Notice how the left and indent margins are set.

- ❏ Type in the text for the point, press **ENTER** and click the next number is automatically incremented.

- ❏ When you have finished the list press **ENTER** and click on the numbering button to stop automatic numbering and reset the indent margin. Save this document as **Fattips**.

exercise 2.10

Start a new document and create the Findings from Market Research list (used previously as an illustration):

- ❏ Type in the heading and first sentence and create a new line using **ENTER.**

- ❏ Click on the bullet button. A bullet will appear and the insertion point will be ready positioned on the left margin. Notice how the left and indent margins are set.

- ❏ Key in the text for that point.

- ❏ Make a new line, to automatically create the bullet for the next point. Repeat for each point. After the last point press **ENTER** and switch off the bulleting by clicking on the bulleting button. Save this document as **Findings.**

activity 2.5 Text Alignment

Alignment is the way in which the text appears between the left and right margins. In Word6 there are four types of alignment and these are left, right, centre and full justification. The type of alignment can be altered by depressing the appropriate button on the formatting toolbar.

The justification may also be chosen using *Format-Paragraph*, Indents and Spacing, and opening the alignment list box in the **Paragraph** dialog box and selecting the type of alignment.

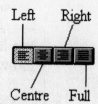

Left alignment causes the text to have a straight left margin and an uneven right margin. The uneven right margin is caused because there is a standard space between each word and each character has a specified amount of space associated with it. If a word does not fit at the end of the line then it is wrapped around onto the next line. This paragraph is written using left alignment and in the diagram of the buttons above, left alignment is shown as being selected.

Centre alignment causes each line of a paragraph to be positioned centrally between the left and right margins. If you use centre alignment while typing the insertion point will start a new line in the centre and the as the left edge of the text moves to the left the insertion point moves to the right. This type of alignment is very useful for titles, title pages, menus and posters.

Right alignment is the opposite of left alignment, so the right margin is straight and the left margin is uneven as demonstrated in this paragraph. Right alignment is used in letters or memos where the address, date or reference number is to appear on the right hand side of the page.

Fully justified alignment is where both the right and the left margins have straight edges. The way that this is done is by the word processor inserting extra gaps into the line so that the words line up at the right hand edge. This type of alignment is commonly chosen for many types of documents.

exercise 2.11

Start a new document to create a front page for the report.

---

the Manchester Metropolitan University
Crewe + Alsager Faculty

Environment & Enterprise Project

The Refurbishment of the Multi-Gym into a Fitness Suite at Chelmer Leisure and Recreation Centre

A Feasibility Study

By: Sarah Leveridge
Tutor: R. S. Symmond
Course: HND Business and Finance
Date: 1st February 1995

- ❑ Select Arial point size 12 for the name of the institution.
- ❑ For the title, select centre alignment by clicking on the appropriate icon.
- ❑ Key in the words Environment & Enterprise Project using Times New Roman, bold, italic, 14pts. Press **ENTER.**
- ❑ For the main title use Times New Roman, bold, 16pts.
- ❑ Select right alignment.
- ❑ Using Arial, italic, 10pts key in the author, tutor, course and date.
- ❑ Save this document as **Front.**

activity 2.6 Line spacing

Line spacing refers to the space between the bottom of one line and the bottom of the next line. Normally text is typed in 'single spacing' i.e. line spacing is one. Word6 automatically adjusts the line height to accommodate the size of the font you are using.

Choose *Format-Paragraph* to alter the line spacing in the document.

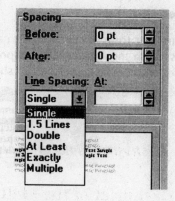

Three types of spacing are listed below.

Single   Single spacing that Word6 can increase depending on the size of font used.

1.5 Lines   One-and-a-half line spacing that Word6 can increase.

Double   Double spacing that Word6 can increase.

exercise 2.12

Into a new document enter the text outlined below.

❑ Using **Format-Paragraph** choose one-and-a-half spacing and key in the first paragraph.

❑ Using **Format-Paragraph** again select double spacing before keying in the second paragraph.

❑ Save this document as **Summary.**

SUMMARY

Chelmer Leisure Centre is one of the facilities of Cheshire Leisure Services. The existing multigym facility has had little money spent on it over the past few years and has experienced a decrease in the number of users. Market research shows that there is a need for this particular facility to be updated.

Three manufacturers of fitness equipment have put forward proposals for

the refurbishment of the multigym into a fitness suite. The proposal chosen

is from Atlanta Sports Industries Ltd. The overall cost for refurbishment will

be £21,000.

Character spacing

There is another form of spacing that can be used and that is spacing between characters. From the Format menu choose Font, click on the Character Spacing 'tab' and open the spacing list box as shown opposite.

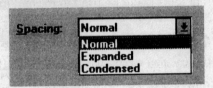

exercise 2.13

Key in the following sentence:

☐ Choose *Format-Font-**Character Spacing***.

☐ Open the **Spacing** box, select **Expanded** and key in the first half of the text up to the word and.

☐ Change to **Normal** spacing using *Format-Font* and type and.

☐ Change to **Condensed** spacing and key in the rest of the sentence.

> E x p a n d e d   s p a c i n g   w i l l   p u t   m o r e   s p a c e   i n   b e t w e e n
> t h e   l e t t e r s   and condensed spacing will reduce the amount of spacing between letters.

integrative exercises

Try to create the following examples which use the formatting techniques discussed in this session.

exercise 2.14 *A private advertisement*

Creating an advertisement for a student notice board. Type the advertisement as follows:

> For Sale – One pair of Ladies Ice Skates, size 6. In very good condition
> as only used one winter. £15 o.n.o.
> Contact Louise Green Room C27 Derby Hall

To make it stand out typefonts could be used.

> **For Sale** – One pair of *Ladies Ice Skates, size 6*. In <u>very good condition</u> as only used one winter. £15 o.n.o.
> Contact **Louise Green** Room C27 Derby Hall

Different fonts could be used to make it more eye-catching.

> **For Sale** – One pair of *Ladies Ice Skates, size 6*. In <u>very good condition</u> as only used one winter. £15 o.n.o.
> Contact Louise Green Room C27 Derby Hall

The last line could be separated from the first paragraph by adjusting the amount of space before it. The first paragraph could have a hanging indent set producing the following effect.

> **For Sale** One pair of *Ladies Ice Skates, size 6*. In <u>very good condition</u> as only used one winter. **£15 o.n.o.**
>
> Contact Louise Green *Room C27* Derby Hall

exercise 2.15 *A business advertisement*

The following advertisement was created using the fonts Arial and Wingdings. All of the text is centre aligned.

A variety of point sizes are used, try point size 18 for the first two lines. Try point size 21, bold for the next two lines.

There is space above the word 'look', use paragraph spacing to adjust this. The hands are created using Wingdings, characters F and E at a point size of 44. Try a point size of 35 for 'look' which is bold, italic.

See if you can create the rest of the advertisement. Consider the typeface, the point size, the space before (or after a paragraph) and character spacing of each line.

TOP-HOLE INSURANCE
BROKERS LIMITED

FOR ALL YOUR
INSURANCE REQUIREMENTS

LOOK
NO FURTHER

**WE CAN INSURE YOUR HOUSEHOLD
CONTENT UP TO £50,000 FOR UNDER
£1.50 PER WEEK**

MOTOR INSURANCE

OVER 25 AND NO PREVIOUS INSURANCE?

If you have held a Full Driving Licence for 4 years with no accidents or convictions

THIRD PARTY – from only £100

FULLY COMPREHENSIVE – from only £150

Call us on (0123) 456789 *NOW!*

---

exercise 2.16 A poster

Create the poster shown below:

☐ Set the left and right margins to 1cm and 13cm respectively.

☐ Choose a suitably sized font and centre align the title.

☐ Set a hanging indent for the question and answer. Move the left margin to 2.5cm. Key in the question and answer text.

☐ Put the left margin back to 1cm. Key in the paragraph of text.

☐ Use centre alignment for the last section.

☐ Check that you have used bold and italics where shown. Save the document as **Poster**, preview and print.

Introducing the
New Generation Bodywrap System

Q.   How does it work?

A.   The Quickslim method of bodywrapping does not depend upon fluid loss through perspiration, but on osmotic activity reducing the inter-cellular fluid.

A course of Quickslim treatment is especially effective when combined with a **G5** treatment and a sensible diet.

See the difference for yourself!

One Wrap £38 – a 90 minute treatment

Discounts available on courses

Contact: Mary at '*The Beauty Room*'

---

objectives

In this session various activities that will aid document production and presentation will be explored. These activities include:

❏ moving and copying text

❏ deleting text

❏ moving quickly around a document

❏ finding and replacing text

❏ checking spelling

❏ making autotext entries

❏ using the thesaurus

❏ using the grammar checker

❏ using Windows

❏ moving text between documents

❏ setting up and using a document template

❏ creating documents of different sizes and orientations

Presentation has an important affect on the reader's initial reactions. When you are producing a document, whether it be for your customers, managers or tutors, good presentation will predispose them to view the document favourably. An important aspect of presentation is sound spelling and grammar. Word provides a range of facilities to assist in improving your documents.

activity 3.1 Moving, copying and deleting text

When a document is being written it is easy to use the word processor to make revisions. Revisions can range from restructuring a sentence to re-arranging the order in which paragraphs appear. The word processor's abilities to move, copy and delete text are an invaluable aid to putting thoughts onto 'electronic' paper!

Moving – cutting and pasting

If a section of the document is out of place, be it a few words, sentences or paragraphs then it can easily be moved to the right place. First select the section to be moved and use *Edit-Cut*, or alternatively click on the **scissors icon** in the **tool bar**.

The selection will disappear from the screen. It is stored in a temporary area in the computer's memory called **the clipboard**. It is important to remember that this is only temporary storage and if anything else is copied to the clipboard then the new overwrites the old. To avoid losing the contents of the clipboard an *Edit-Cut* operation should be followed by an *Edit-Paste* operation as soon as possible.

 To insert the information from the clipboard into the document, first position the insertion point at the correct place within the document and use *Edit-Paste* or click on the **paste icon** in the **tool bar**.

exercise 3.1

With a new document open type in the following sentence.

> The local government environment is changing fast with new laws and new standards appearing almost every month.

❑ Select the portion 'with new laws and new standards appearing almost every month'.

❑ Using *Edit-Cut* will remove this portion and place it on the clipboard.

❑ Move the insertion point to the beginning of the sentence and use *Edit-Paste*.

❑ Tidy up the sentence so that it now reads:

> With new laws and new standards appearing almost every month the local government environment is changing fast.

Moving – dragging and dropping

This is a method of moving which is ideally suited to small selections and small movements, for example, rewording a sentence. First select the section to be moved and then click on the selection and hold down the mouse button. As the pointer is dragged notice that at the bottom of the arrow is a small grey rectangle and also there is a small grey insertion point which follows the pointer movements. This insertion point is the position at which the selection will be dropped when the mouse button is released.

exercise 3.2

Type in the following sentence:

> If you wish to reserve a place complete and return the reply slip overleaf please.

Highlight the word please and the space before it and drag the insertion marker to the end of place. Release the button and the sentence should read:

> If you wish to reserve a place please complete and return the reply slip overleaf.

Copying and pasting

This is very similar to Cut and Paste except that the selected text remains in the document and a copy of it is placed on the clipboard. The copy that is in the clipboard is available to be pasted into the document.

First select the section to be copied and use *Edit-Copy* or click on the copy icon in the tool bar. Position the insertion point at the place in the document where the copy is to go and use *Edit-Paste* or click on the **paste** icon. The contents of the clipboard may be pasted into the document as many times as required.

Deleting

Normal deleting as a running correction can be achieved using either the **BACK-SPACE** or the **DELETE** key. However, if a larger portion of the document needs to be deleted then it may be selected and then removed by pressing the **DELETE** key.

Undoing

Remember that, in any of the above activities if the desired change does not occur use *Edit-Undo* straight away and try again. *Edit-Undo* will undo your last action. Alternatively click on the **undo icon**. If you wish to undo more than one action use the undo drop-down list.

exercise 3.3

Start a new document and key in the following text. Save it as **Centre**.

INTRODUCTION

The Chelmer Leisure and Recreation Centre is at present a very basic gym. It is used by people from a wide range of socio-economic backgrounds. The majority of people using the centre come from the surrounding catchment area.

It is proposed to apply for Local Council funding for refurbishing the present multigym facility into a fitness suite. In recent years little money has been spent on the multigym. This has resulted in a decrease in the number of users. Present users of the multigym are weightlifters most of whom are male.

The fitness centre offers a wide range of activities. The centre is also an extremely popular venue for aerobics, step classes, keep fit and popmobility. These classes are responsible for attracting a large number of female users to the centre, who, in the event of refurbishment of the multigym, would be a large target group. The aerobic based activities account for nearly half of the total number of users of the centre. It is hoped that with the introduction of a fitness suite, those existing users will also use the new facility.

Using *Edit-Cut* and *Edit-Paste* reword the first sentence of the last paragraph to read 'A wide range of activities is offered by the fitness centre'.

❏ First select the part of the sentence 'a wide range of activities' and use *Edit-Cut*.

❏ Move the insertion point to the beginning of the sentence and use *Edit-Paste*.

❏ The sentence requires some tidying up, make the first word a capital A. An alternative way in which to change the case of a word is to select it and press **SHIFT+F3**.

❏ Put a space after **activities** and type the word **is**.

❏ Select the word **offers**, use *Edit-Cut*, position the insertion point after **is**, use *Edit-Paste* and change **offers** to **offered by**.

❏ Make the T in **The** lower case and remove the space before the full stop.

❏ Reword the fourth sentence to read 'Nearly half of the total number of users of the centre take part in aerobic based activities'. Save the amended document.

activity 3.2 Moving quickly around a document

Normally you move around a document by moving the insertion point. The insertion point can be moved using the ARROW keys or by moving the mouse pointer to a certain point and clicking. There are also a number of ways to move quickly to another part of the document. These are summarised in the table below:

Key Combination	Result
HOME	Moves insertion point to the start of the current line.
END	Moves insertion point to the end of the current line.
PAGE UP and PAGE DOWN	Move either up or down by one screen height. The insertion point generally remains in the same position on the screen, however, it is in a different part of the document.
CTRL + HOME	Moves the insertion point to the beginning of the document.
CTRL + END	Moves the insertion point to the end of the document.
CTRL + PAGE UP	Moves the insertion point to the top left hand corner of the current screen.
CTRL + PAGE DOWN	Moves the insertion point to the bottom right hand corner of the current screen.
CTRL + ←	Moves the insertion point to the beginning of the current word.
CTRL + →	Moves the insertion point to the beginning of the next word.
CTRL + G (*Edit-Go to*)	Moves to a particular page in the document. Enter the required page number into the dialog box.

Using the scroll bars

There are scroll bars to the right and the bottom of the document window. Using the scroll bars will allow up, down, left or right movement around the document.

By clicking on the box with an arrow at either end of the scroll bar a small movement in the direction of the arrow will be made. By dragging the scroll box to another position in the scroll bar larger movements can be made. Clicking in the vertical scroll bar has the effect of **PAGE UP** or **PAGE DOWN** depending which side of the scroll box you click. Clicking in the horizontal scroll bar causes movements of a screen width. Note that when scrolling the insertion point remains static.

activity 3.3 Finding and replacing text

The ability to search through a document and find a particular section of text or 'string', and if required replace it with another, is an extremely useful feature. There are varied uses for **Find** and **Find and Replace,** an example for each follows.

By using **Find and Replace** a mistake such as an incorrectly spelt company name can be corrected throughout a document. **Find** is useful in proof-reading, for example, finding a topic name such as 'fitness centre' will enable all parts of the document that deal with aspects this topic to be found. This helps to ensure consistency throughout a document.

Find and Replace

Finding and Replacing allows a particular string to be located and to be replaced by an alternative string. ***Edit-Replace*** is used to invoke the replace facility and the **Replace** dialog box appears:

In the **Find What** box enter the text string to be located. This text string may be part of a word, a whole word or several words. In the **Replace With** box enter the replacement string. Replacing works for all the document, from the insertion point to the beginning or from the insertion point to the end of the document depending upon whether, All, Up or Down is selected in the **Search** box.

If the search string being used is a single word which could also form part of a larger word then the **Find Whole Words Only** option may be selected. If the aim is to find all the whole words and any words that contain the search string then leave the check box blank. Click on this option to put a cross in the check box if the aim is only to find the whole word.

Normal searching is not case sensitive so searching for the string **the** will find the, The, THE etc. and any words containing the, The, and THE. To make the search case sensitive click on the **Match Case** option.

A form of special matching that can be used with both **Find** and **Replace,** is to be able to search for any character. To do this choose the **Use Pattern** Matching option. For example, typing **place?** in the **Find What** box will find, place, replace, placement.

Once the search string has been found there are three replacement options available.

❑ To replace the search string with the replace string click on the **Replace** button.

❑ To skip to the next occurrence of the search string without replacing it click on the **Find Next** button.

❑ To replace all occurrences of the search string with the replace string click on **Replace All.**

Note: **Replace All** option should be used with utmost caution. Unintentional replacements may occur especially if the search string forms part of other words.

Find

To search for a particular string choose *Edit-Find*. This will produce a dialog box:

In the **Find What** box enter the text string to be located. Press **ENTER** and then click on the **Find Next** button to find the next occurrence of the specified string. To find the next occurrence click on the **Find Next** button again. The direction of the search may be controlled by the choice of the **Search** option.

exercise 3.4

Into a new document, key in the following text. Save this document as **Usage.**

Usage of the centre

Chelmer Leisure Centre is a fairly small centre which offers no 'wet' sporting activities. The centre does not have sauna or solarium facilities. Approximately a mile away there is a swimming pool which offers these facilities.

The centre is well used. In a recent eight month period over 26 thousand people passed through the centre. On average over three thousand people per month are using the facilities offered by the centre. This gives an average daily figure of over 100 people. However, demand fluctuates depending on the day of the week and whether it was a holiday period.

Popular activities offered by the centre are Step, Popmobility, Keep fit and Aerobics. The figures for people attending these over the eight month period studied are Step 5058, Popmobility 4779, Keep Fit 679 and Aerobics 2080.

The total number of people attending these activities account for nearly half the total number of people using the Leisure centre over the eight month period studied.

To use the **Replace** facility:

❏ Position the insertion point at the beginning of the first paragraph.

❏ Use *Edit-Replace* and in the **Find What** box type **people** and in the **Replace With** box type **clients.**

❏ Click on **Find Next** and use **Replace**. The word people will be replaced by clients and Word will find the next occurrence of people.

❏ Repeat the **Replace** command to replace all occurrences of people with clients.

❏ Reposition the insertion point at the beginning of the first paragraph.

❏ Use *Edit-Replace* and in the **Find What** box type **studied** and in the **Replace With** box type **analysed.**

❏ Click on **Find Next** and skip the first occurrence using **Find Next**. This time use the **Replace** command to replace the remaining occurrences of studied with analysed.

Extra features in finding and replacing

In both the **Find** and the **Replace** dialog boxes there is a **Format** button. This allows a search string to be defined very specifically in terms of its font, colour and the formatting applied to it.

For example, it is possible to search for the word text where the font is Times New Roman, size 14 and colour green and where it appears in a paragraph that is centre justified.

Finding and replacing special characters

Word allows for many special characters to be located and replaced. A special character is one which usually has an invisible effect upon the document. Examples of special characters include the **TAB** character, paragraph mark and page break. Special characters can be made to show by clicking on the **special character icon**. Clicking this icon again will cause them to disappear.

For example, suppose a piece of text is imported into Word which was originally created by another word processor. At the end of every line regardless or not of whether it is the end of a sentence or paragraph there is a new line character. In Word a new line character or paragraph mark is only necessary at the end of paragraphs.

To allow Word to perform word-wrapping on this piece of text the superfluous paragraph marks will need to be removed. Some will be kept, that is, those which mark the end of each paragraph.

This task can be performed by using *Edit-Replace*. Click on the **Special** button and select Paragraph mark from the list and **^p** appears in the **Find What** box. Leave the **Replace with** box empty and click on the **Replace** button where a replacement is required and click on the **Find Next** button where a replacement is not required i.e. where there are ends of paragraphs.

Some of the special characters you may wish to use are, **^t** for TAB characters and **^d** for non-automatic (or hard) page breaks.

exercise 3.5

Open the document, **Usage,** from the previous exercise and click on the **special character icon**. If you have a paragraph marker at the end of every line you have not been using word wrap properly. Read Activity 1.1 again. Note which other special characters are displayed. Click on the **special character icon** to remove the special characters from the display.

activity 3.4 Improving text

There are various ways in which the word processor can help to improve the text in a document. Many word processor users are not trained typists and are prone to make errors while keying in their work. So it is useful to be able to check for mistakes, particularly spelling. However, the word processor cannot proof-read a document so after checking the spelling and grammar always proof-read your work. If the work would benefit from re-wording use the thesaurus to help.

Using the spell checker

The spell checker can be used to check a selection or the whole document. If a selection is to be checked, select it first. Use *Tools-Spelling* or click on the

Spelling icon or use the shortcut key F7. If you have not made a selection Word will start the spell check from the position of the insertion point.

The **Spelling** dialog box appears

When the spell checker comes across a word it does not recognise it shows it in the **Not in Dictionary** box. In the **Change To** box the spell checker offers a correction. If there are more than one possible corrections these are listed in the **Suggestions** box. Behind the spelling dialog box the document can be seen with the word in question highlighted.

There are now a number of options available, shown by the buttons

❑ If the **Change To** box contains the correct spelling click on the **Change** button.

❑ If the correct spelling is in the **Suggestions** box click on it to put it into the **Change To** box and click on the **Change** button.

❑ If you think that the mistake may be repeated throughout the document then use the **Change All** button instead of the **Change** button.

❑ If the word is correct but it is not in the spell checker's dictionary then choose **Ignore** or you may **Add** the word to your own dictionary. Consult the Help files or manual for information about creating your own dictionary. Use **Ignore All** to ignore all occurrences of the word throughout the document.

If a selection is not made, the spell checker will check the entire document, and when finished will return to the original place of the insertion point. If you are checking a selection, when that is finished you have the option to carry on and check the whole document.

AutoCorrect

As you type Word will monitor your typing for common mistakes. Word maintains a list of 'mistypes' and their corrections and will correct you if you mistype a word in its list, for example the word 'the'. If you do not wish Word to do this then you can switch off this feature using ***Tools-AutoCorrect*** and remove the x from the **Replace Text As You Type** check box.

You may add 'mistype' words and their corrections to the AutoCorrect list, either through using *Tools-AutoCorrect* or by clicking on the **AutoCorrect** button in the **Spelling** dialog box.

exercise 3.6

For this exercise, in checking spelling, open the document **Centre.**

❐ Click on the spell check icon and check your spelling.

❐ If you correct any errors save the document before closing it.

❐ Try this with other files you have created e.g. **Usage, Termref** and **Qdesign.**

Using the thesaurus

The thesaurus can be used to add variety and interest to your work. A thesaurus finds synonyms and related words. The Thesaurus is used for one word at a time. Place the insertion point in the appropriate word and then choose *Tools-Thesaurus*.

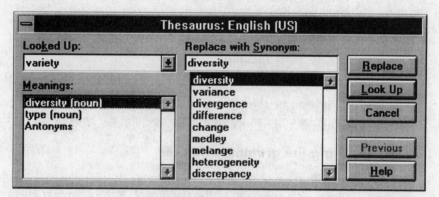

The word that was selected appears in the **Looked Up** box. Underneath this is the **Meanings** box which lists related words and indicates whether these words are nouns or verbs. Next to the **Looked Up** box is a **Replace with Synonyms** box which contains a list of synonyms for the selected word. You can replace the selected word with any of the words listed by clicking on the word. It will then appear in the text box at the top of the list and clicking on the **Replace** button will put it into the document in place of the word selected.

If the list of synonyms is not extensive enough then the Thesaurus can be used to find synonyms for the word in the **Looked Up** box. To do this click on the **LOOK UP** button. This procedure may be repeated until a suitable synonym is found.

The Thesaurus keeps a list of all the words you have looked up. To return to a previous word open the **Looked Up** list box, by clicking on the arrow at the end of the box. Words which you have previously looked up are displayed and the required word can be chosen from the list.

exercise 3.7

Key the following text into a new document and save it as **Promote.**

Chelmer Leisure and Recreation Centre has a small promotional budget which the management can use as they see fit. In the event of a new fitness suite being opened at the centre a great deal of effort must be channelled into creating awareness of the new facility to the potential customer.

The centre is a local authority facility which opens up a range of areas for promotional activities. Other local amenities provide excellent space to promote the new facility. Libraries, other sports facilities, Town Halls and Theatres are venues where any promotional material advertising the new facility can be placed.

Local papers are an excellent promotional tool in the area. There are two popular local papers which are issued weekly and circulated throughout the area. These are the Herald, which is sold throughout the Borough and the Advertiser which is a free newspaper.

Using the Thesaurus investigate synonyms for the following words, deal, creating, range, popular.

❏ Place the insertion point in the word to be investigated.

❏ Use **Tools-Thesaurus.**

❏ Consider whether a replacement should be selected from the list of synonyms.

❏ Investigate the effect of 'looking up' a word. Remember that a list of words looked up can be viewed by opening the **Looked Up** list box.

Using the grammar checker

As with the spell checker the grammar checker can check either the whole document or a selection of the document. If the grammar checker finds a sentence with questionable grammar or style, it displays it in the dialog box as shown below.

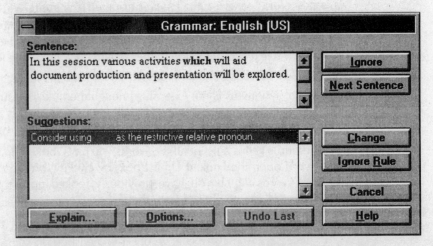

Words related to the suspected error are displayed in red type. The grammar checker displays suggested corrections in the **Suggestions** box. Choices of action are:

❐ Make a suggested correction.

❐ Select one of the corrections from the **Suggestions** box and click on the **Change** button. If the **Change** button is unavailable i.e. it is in grey, then type the correction directly into the document. This can occur if the Grammar command has suggested a change which is too complex for it to undertake.

❐ Make your own corrections in the document.

❐ Make the document window active by clicking on it. Edit the sentence and click on the **Start** button in the dialog box to resume checking the document.

❐ Ignore the questioned word or sentence without making changes.

❐ Click on the **Ignore** button.

❐ Skip the entire sentence.

❐ Click on the **Next Sentence** button to start checking the next sentence.

❐ Ask for an explanation of the error.

❐ Click on the **Explain** button, press **ESC** to return to the grammar check. For explanation of grammatical rules refer to the user manual.

❐ Customise the grammatical rules used for checking.

❐ Click on the **Options** button. Refer to user manual for the grammatical rules that are available.

exercise 3.8

The following piece of text is deliberately incorrect. Key it into a new document exactly. Move the insertion point to the beginning and use *Tools-Grammar.* Note that before grammar checking Word does a spell check.

Atlanta's proposal were the one considered the most attractive for Chelmer Leisure and Recreation Centre. The Athena equipment offer a great advantage due to the nature of it's design. There equipment is designed so that it can be positioned 'back to back' to save valuable space.

After the spelling check is complete, the first sentence is highlighted and a suggestion for correction offered:

❐ Click on the second suggestion (consider **was** instead of **were**)

❐ Click on the **Change** button.

❐ Highlight the second suggestion (consider **offers** instead of **offer**) and click on **Change**.

❐ Change **it's** into **its** and **There** into **Their.**

The final sentence is also highlighted as it contains a verb in the passive voice. It is not necessary to make a change but if you wish to do so:

❑ Click on **Explain** to see an example of what is meant by passive voice. Close this window using its control menu button.

❑ Click on the document, the **Grammar** window becomes inactive. Make changes so that the first part of the sentence reads 'Their equipment design is such that...'

❑ Click on the **Grammar** dialog box to make it active and click on **Start.**

❑ The second part of the sentence contains a verb in passive voice but this time ignore the rule by clicking on **Ignore.**

activity 3.5 Using the AutoText

The activities described in this section are aimed at reducing the amount of keying that might be performed in producing a document. If you have used Word2 you may be more familiar with the term glossary instead of autotext.

Creating AutoText entries

Word uses AutoText to save repeated keying of the same text. Some documents contain text (and/or graphics) which is repeated several or many times. For example, a company name, address or logo may appear several times in one document or may be required in many documents. By defining the name, address or logo as an AutoText entry it may be recalled at any point in any document with a simple keying action. Take a simple example, the text *Yours sincerely* appears at the end of many business letters. If many letters are to be typed then defining this as an AutoText entry would help to save time keying.

Word maintains a list of AutoText entries which you can add to or delete from. An AutoText entry may be text, graphics or a mixture of text and graphics. You can save text or graphics that you use often as an AutoText entry. Then you can easily insert the text or graphics into a document with a simple keying action, rather than retyping or using copy and paste.

Making an AutoText entry

First type in the text that you intend to make into an AutoText entry. Check spelling is correct and select the text. Choose *Edit-AutoText,* and the **AutoText** dialog box appears:

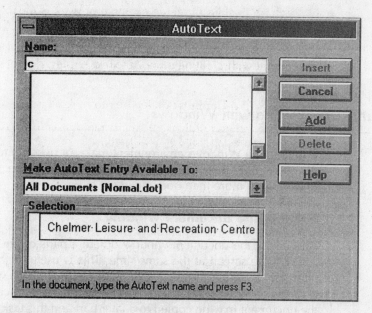

in the **Name** box type a name for the AutoText entry, in this example **c** for Chelmer Leisure and Recreation Centre. Then click on the **Add** button.

Using an AutoText entry

The simplest method of using an AutoText entry is to type the AutoText name followed immediately by **F3** (function key 3) i.e. typing **c** and pressing **F3** would produce the text Chelmer Leisure and Recreation Centre.

Alternatively, if you forget your AutoText names (for example, ys could be the glossary name for Yours sincerely) then use *Edit-AutoText*, in the dialog box will be a list of your previously defined AutoText entries. Type or select the Autotext name you wish to use and click on the **Insert** button.

exercise 3.9

Open a new document and try setting up and using the following AutoText entries:

AutoText name	AutoText entry
ys	Yours sincerely
yf	Yours faithfully
ms	Microsoft Word

❏ Type out the AutoText entry in full e.g. Yours sincerely

❏ Select this text

❏ Use *Edit-AutoText* and in the **Name** box type the AutoText name e.g. ys

❏ Click on **Add**

❏ Move the insertion point to a place where the AutoText entry is to appear

❏ Type the AutoText name e.g. ys and press **F3**

Experiment with creating other AutoText entries, do not save this document.

activity **3.6** Working with Windows

Working in a Windows environment makes it possible for different portions of a document to be viewed on the screen at the same time. It also makes it possible to work with more than one document at once.

Splitting the document window

By splitting the document window different parts of the same document can be seen on the screen at the same time. This is useful if the portion being written refers to an earlier portion. Viewing the earlier portion while writing the current portion can save scrolling up and down through the document. An earlier part of the document may be copied to a later part and this task is simplified by viewing both parts of the document on screen at the same time.

To split the document:

❏ Move the mouse pointer to the black bar at the top of the vertical scroll bar. The pointer changes shape to two horizontal lines with arrows.

❏ While the pointer is this shape click and drag a horizontal line downwards. Position the line approximately half-way down the document window and release.

At the right hand edge of the window the vertical scroll bar now appears as two separate scroll bars, one for each portion of the split. It is possible to scroll each split portion independently thereby positioning an earlier portion of the document on the screen at the same time as a later one.

To remove a split:

❏ Move the mouse pointer to the black bar between the two vertical scroll bars. The pointer changes shape to two horizontal lines with arrows.

❏ While the pointer is this shape click and drag the split line upwards. Position the line at the top of the document screen area and release.

More than one window onto the same document

Another way of viewing two parts of a document at the same time is to use more than one window. This can provide more flexibility and be useful when working with larger documents. If, for example, you wished to refer to more than one page of the document then it would be useful to be able to switch between several 'views' of the different pages.

To set up another window onto the document use *Window-New Window*. Word displays the beginning of the document and the title of the document has been altered by the addition of a **:2**. This is the window number. Every time *Window-New Window* is used a new window onto the document is created.

To see a list of the windows that have been created open the *Window* menu. The list of open windows is in the lower section of this menu. To switch to another window simply click on the name of the appropriate one in the *Window* list.

File-Close closes the document and all associated windows. To close a document's specific windows use the control menu box associated with that window.

To view several windows on the screen at the same time use *Windows-Arrange All*. The windows can be positioned by moving and sizing them, however, the screen can become rather cluttered. For this reason it is advisable to have no more than four windows open. Only one window can be active at once, if the default Windows colours are being used then the active window has a blue title bar. To alter the active window simply click on the one to be made active.

Cutting and copying between windows

Copy or Cut and Paste operations can be carried out between windows. First switch to or make active the window containing the portion of the document which is to be cut or copied. Select the section and *Edit-Cut* or *Edit-Copy* it to the clipboard.

Next switch to or make active, by clicking in it, the window into which the contents of the clipboard are to be pasted. Position the insertion point and *Edit-Paste*.

Working with more than one document

All that has been described about using more than one window into a document can be applied to using more than one document. Instead of using *Window-New Window* to open more windows onto the document, use *File-Open* to open all the documents required. To see a list of all open documents open the *Window* menu, and use *Window-Arrange All* if you wish to see all windows on the screen at the same time.

Copy or cut and paste operations can be carried out as previously described. Note that portions that are pasted into a document retain the font and formatting that was applied in the original document.

exercise 3.10

To perform this exercise close any documents that you may have open using *File-Close.* When all documents are closed only the **File** and **Help** menus are available on the menu bar.

❏ Open the file **Termref**

- ❐ Open the file **Centre**

- ❐ Choose *Window-Arrange All.* Both documents should be visible on the screen each occupying its own window which takes up half the screen display.

- ❐ Open the file **Usage.** Open the *Window* menu and notice that all the open documents are listed. Select *Arrange-All.*

The screen has become cluttered so close **Termref**:

- ❐ Click anywhere in the **Termref** document window to make it active.

- ❐ Click on the control menu box for that window and chose *Close.* Use *Window-Arrange All* to re-position the remaining document windows.

To copy text from one window to another:

- ❐ Make **Centre** active by clicking in its window. Press **CTRL+END** to move the insertion point to the end of the document.

- ❐ Make **Usage** active.

- ❐ Highlight the first paragraph and use *Edit-Copy.*

- ❐ Make **Centre** active, the insertion point should be at the end of the document, and use *Edit-Paste.*

- ❐ Close the documents but do not save the changes.

activity 3.7 Creating Templates

A template is a pre-defined format for a document. Many business documents such as letters, memos, forms and reports have set formats. A template can be used to define not only standard text but also aspects such as the font, borders, page size and orientation. Once a template has been created it can be recalled and used to produce the required document. This saves time and ensures consistency.

Word comes with several pre-defined templates. To create most documents the template called NORMAL.DOT is used. This is the template that you have been using to create your documents. If a document is started using *File-New* then a dialog box containing the names of the templates appears. By choosing NORMAL you are in fact selecting a template file. Template files have the extension .dot and are stored in the word directory.

Word provides other template files such as a standard letter and memo and it is possible to customise these. However, this activity will concentrate on producing a custom template based on the normal template. The template will contain standard text. Standard text is often referred to as boilerplate text.

exercise 3.11

There are several ways of creating a template, the one that will be used for this exercise is to create a template from the document that is being worked on. The template will be set up based upon Word's normal template which is the one usually used for document creation. Start a new document and key in the following text, leaving the prices blank.

Chelmer Leisure and Recreation Centre
MultiGym

Price per session

Adult
Junior
Concessionary
Club Adult
Club Junior

Save this as a template rather than a document. Use **File-Save**, in the **File-Save** dialog box open the **Save File as Type** box and choose **Document Template**. Type a file name, **Price,** into the **File Name** box and click OK.

To use this template for the creation of a new document (e.g. when the prices change):

❒ Start a new document using **File-New.**

❒ Select from the **Template** dialog box choose the name of the template just created (**Price**).

❒ The (boilerplate) text and formatting will appear and the prices can be filled in and the document saved and printed in the usual manner.

Template files can be recalled and edited, but remember to select **Document Template** in the **List Files of Type** box in the **File-Open** dialog box. Template files are normally stored in the Word sub-directory not in your working directory. Word automatically changes directory to find the template files when they are requested through the **List Files of Type** box. If you use a networked version of Word then custom templates may be stored in an alternative directory. Check with your network manager.

integrative exercises

exercise 3.12 *Find and Replace*

Type the following paragraph into a new document.

> The mouse is a hand-held device connected to a computer which can be used as an alternative to the keyboard for issuing commands or instructions. Its shape resembles a mouse with a cable for a tail and buttons for eyes. Unlike a real mouse the cable emerges from between the eyes! The operator's hand grips the mouse between thumb and little finger allowing the first and second fingers rest over the buttons.
>
> Sliding the mouse over the desk top, ideally using a mouse mat, beside the computer, rotates a direction sensitive ball inside which in turn causes a pointer to move around the screen.
>
> Commands are chosen from an on-screen menu by pointing to them with the tip of the pointer and usually 'clicking' the left-hand button.
>
> In painting applications the pointer can be used as a drawing tool such as a paintbrush. On a colour monitor a palette of colours is available and selecting from the palette puts paint on the paintbrush. It is usual to be able to alter the thickness of the line painted by the paintbrush. There may also be an air-brush tool which creates a spray painting effect.

- ❐ Position the insertion point at the top of the document.
- ❐ Using *Edit-Find* and, searching down through the text, find every instance of the word paint.
- ❐ Position the insertion point at the end of the document
- ❐ Use *Edit-Find* to find the word mouse, searching up through the text.
- ❐ Repeat the search to find every instance of the whole word paint.
- ❐ Using *Edit-Replace* change the word mouse to rodent.

exercise 3.13 *Defining and using an AutoText entry*

Add the following paragraph to the document **Promote** created in Exercise 3.7.

- ❐ After typing **new fitness suite** select it
- ❐ Use *Edit-AutoText* to define it as an AutoText entry with the name **n**.
- ❐ Next time this needs to be keyed in simply type n followed by **F3**.

> This form of advertising i.e. posters, advertisements in local papers offers a direct link with the public. The money which is spent now to promote the new fitness suite is done so in the hope of increasing usage. The outcome of this form of promotion is uncertain but the main aims are to:
>
> - Create awareness of the new fitness suite
> - Inform the public of the services on offer at the centre
> - Educate/inform of the benefits of the new fitness suite

objectives

This session focuses on activities associated with the creation of tables of text and numbers. At the end of this session you will be able to:

- ❏ use **tab stops** to set up a simple table
- ❏ use the **table feature** to develop a more extensive table
- ❏ **put existing text into a table**
- ❏ apply **borders** and **shading** to text

Familiarity with such operations will allow you to construct documents where it is frequently necessary to present text or numbers in columns, such as tables of numbers or text, curriculum vitae, questionnaires and forms.

It is frequently necessary to be able to present text or numbers as lists in columns. If you are accustomed to using a typewriter you may have used the **SPACEBAR** to align text. **Do NOT use the SPACEBAR** to format or align text with a word processor. The **SPACEBAR** should only be used to insert a space between words. If you attempt to use the **SPACEBAR** to align text in columns, this will impede later formatting and although columns may appear aligned on the screen they will not be aligned when printed out. Modern printers use proportionally spaced fonts where different letters are allocated different amounts of space. It is essential to use the facilities described in this Session in order to produce effective tables.

Often tables contain figures and Word offers the facility to manipulate these in a 'spreadsheet-like' way, for example, to total a column. The third activity in Session 9 introduces this aspect of tables.

activity 4.1 Working with tab stops

Using default tab stops

The simplest way to create text that is lined up in columns is to use tab stops. If you inspect the Ruler, by selecting *View-Ruler*, you will see that Word provides default left tab stops at every half inch. Text can be aligned at these tab stops simply by pressing the TAB key to move to the next tab stop position.

The default tab stops can be changed by choosing **Format-Tabs**, and making appropriate changes in the **Default Tab Stops** box, and then choosing **OK**.

exercise 4.1

With a new document open:

☐ type in the following text, working one line at a time and using the **TAB** key to move between one column and the next.

☐ Press the **ENTER** key to move on to a new line.

☐ Finally format the headings as shown in the sample.

```
Opening Times

Health Suite

Monday      9.00am - 9.00pm      Ladies Only
Tuesday     9.00am - 9.00pm      Mixed
Wednesday   9.30am - 9.00pm      Mixed
Thursday    9.00am - 1.00pm      Ladies Only
            1.00pm - 9.00pm      Mixed
Friday      9.00am - 9.00pm      Men Only
Saturday    9.00am - 1.00pm      Men Only
            1.00pm - 5.00pm      Mixed
Sunday      9.00am - 5.00pm      Mixed
```

Now change the default tab stops so that the final column is further away from the times, by choosing *Format-Tabs* and using the **Default Tab Stops** box and increasing the distance between the default tab stops, and notice the effect on your document. Save this document as **Times**.

Types of Tab Stops

There are four types of tab stops: left, centre, right and decimal. Each of these may be set by clicking on the Tab button on the ruler, which in the default mode is shown as a left tab. Clicking on this button, causes it to cycle the different tab types.

Tab Stops

Tab button	Tab type	Tab function
	Left	Text is aligned with its left edge on the tab stops; this is the usual typewriter type of tab and is the default. This is useful for aligning columns of words.
	Centre	Text is centred beneath the tab stop. This can be useful in adverts and other documents where you wish to display text.

Right   Text is aligned with its right edge under the tab stop. This is useful for numbers that do not contain a decimal point and for text that must be aligned in a column, against, say, the right margin.

 Decimal   Numbers are aligned with the decimal point beneath the tab stop. Clearly useful for numbers and, particularly money.

Setting tab stops with the ruler and the mouse

It is easiest in the first instance if you insert tab stops before creating text, rather than try to add them later, although this is perfectly possible once you are confident with the use of tab stops.

To add a tab stop:

❑ select the paragraphs to which you want to add tab stops, or position the insertion point where you want the formatting with tab stops to start, as you type the document.

❑ click on one of the tab button until it displays the tab type that you wish to use e.g. left, right, centre or decimal.

❑ point to where you wish to place the tab on the ruler and click to place a tab stop at that point. The tab should appear on the ruler as a tiny version of the tab symbol on the button.

This procedure can be repeated to add other tab stops.

Ruler without custom tab stops, the default tabs can just be seen on the lower part of the ruler at half inch intervals.

Ruler showing custom tabs. There is a left tab at 1.5cm, a centre tab at 4.5cm, a right tab at 7.5cm and a decimal tab at 11.5cm.

Clearing custom tab stops with the ruler

To clear custom tab stops:

❑ select the paragraph that contains the tab stops to be cleared.

❑ on the ruler drag the marker for the tab stop that you want to remove down out of the ruler

Customising tab stops with the Tabs command

The *Tabs* command offers a further way of controlling various aspects of tab stops. With the appropriate paragraph selected, choose *Format-Tabs*, or double click on any tab stop marker on the ruler. This displays the **Tabs** dialog box:

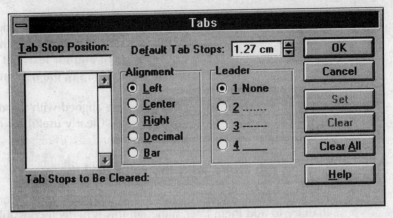

This box allows you to change the format of existing tabs or to add any new tabs. Formatting will be applied to the tab displayed in the box at the top of the **Tab stop position** box. You can enter a new tab position in this box, or display an existing tab by selecting it from further down the **Tab stop position** box. For each tab it is possible to set its alignment and leader. A leader is a series of characters that appear before the text at the tab stop, such as a series of dots. After specifying these characteristics, click on the **SET** button. The position of the default stops may be adjusted and, stops may be cleared using the **CLEAR** or **CLEAR ALL** buttons. Exit with **OK** to accept new settings.

exercise 4.2

With the document called **Times** open that you used in Exercise 4.1, move the pointer to the end of the existing text and reset the tabs to cater for the following text. You should set the following tabs as indicated below:

❏ a left tab at 1.00" (2.5cm)

❏ a centre tab at 2.50" (6.5cm)

❏ a right tab at 4.00" (10.25cm)

Health Suite Passcards

Gold Passcard. Use of all our facilities including the Health Suite, Fitness Suite , Pool and Oasis.

```
3 Month     Gold Pass        £85.00
6 Month     Gold Pass       £150.00
12 Month    Gold Pass       £275.00
```

❏ Click on the **TAB** button on the ruler and choose the appropriate tab type.

❏ Point to where you wish to place the tab on the ruler and click to place a tab stop at that point.

❏ Type in the text, using the **TAB** key to move between tab stops.

Now re-format the tabs:

❏ Select the text that you have just entered and use the *Format-Tabs* command, to display the **Tabs** dialog box on screen.

❏ Select the first tab, change its alignment to **Right** and introduce a leader with ....

❏ Choose **SET**, then **OK**.

❏ Reformat the third tab using *Format-Tabs*. Change its alignment to Decimal.

❏ Note the effect that this has on your document.

Save this document as **Times**.

exercise 4.3

This exercise asks you to insert a new paragraph with new tabs in the middle of a document. Newcomers to word processing often have difficulty with this, so it is worth practising.

With the document called **Times** open:

❏ move the insertion point to a position between the two pieces of text that you entered for Exercise 4.1 and 4.2, respectively.

❏ Open up some space by pressing **ENTER**.

❏ Move the insertion point back to the top of this space.

❏ prepare to insert the following table:

```
Fitness Suite


Monday        8.00am - 8.00pm
              8.00pm - 9.00pm       Super Circuit
Tuesday       9.00am - 9.00pm
Wednesday     9.30am - 8.00pm
              8.00am - 9.00pm       Super Circuit
Thursday      9.00am - 9.00pm
Friday        9.00am - 9.00pm
Saturday      9.00am - 5.00pm
Sunday        9.00am - 5.00pm
```

❏ Set a centre tab at 5cm (2″) and a left tab at 9cm (3.10″) using the ruler.

❏ Enter text using the **TAB** key to move between at stops.

❏ Now move up and down the document and examine the different tab stops as they are applied to different parts of the document.

❏ Save the document as **Times** and close **Times**.

activity 4.2 Setting up a table

Tables are an easy way to arrange and adjust columns of text and numbers, and are much more flexible than tabs. Once you have taken a few moments to master tables you will wonder how you ever managed without them. A table can be inserted at any point in your text. A table offers an easy way to group paragraphs side by side and to arrange text beside related graphics on a page. Tables can be used to organise information in the data documents that are merged to create form letters, mailing labels and other merged documents. By adding borders and shading to a table you can create many types of forms. Tables allow easy transfer of data between Excel and Word. If you create a table in Word, you can insert the table in an Excel worksheet and work with it as you would with any other spreadsheet data; the converse is also possible. Insert an Excel worksheet into a Word document and you can work with the data just as you would with a Word table. However, more of these ambitious applications of tables later.

This activity demonstrates how you can set-up and work with tables.

Setting up a simple table

To set up a table:

- ❏ position the insertion point where you want to insert the table.
- ❏ click on the **TABLE** button on the toolbar.
- ❏ On the Table button grid, drag the pointer to select the number of columns and rows that you want the new table to have.
- ❏ Release the mouse button to insert the table.

or

- ❏ Choose *Table-Insert Table*.
- ❏ In the **Number of Columns** box, type or select a number indicating how many columns you want.
- ❏ Choose **OK**.

Note: You can add rows and adjust column widths later to suit your needs. It is usually a good idea to accept the defaults on your first try.

Entering Text in a table

Once you have created a table, you should have an empty table, with the insertion point in the first cell so that you can start typing. Mostly you can move the insertion point and select and edit text in the same way as in the rest of your document. As you enter text the boxes will expand to accommodate text.

Table Operations

To	Operation
Start new paragraphs in a cell	Press **ENTER**
move to the next cell	Press **TAB**
move to the first cell in the next row	Press **TAB** in the rightmost cell
Add another row of cells	Press **TAB** in the last cell in the table
leave the table	Place the insertion point after the table before typing
Insert a **TAB** stop	With the pointer in the box in which you wish to insert a TAB stop, click on the Tab stop button to select the type of tab stop, then whilst depressing CTRL, click on the ruler where you wish to insert the tab stop.
Change the column width	Drag the cell border on the right side of the column whose width you want to change

Note: When you create a table, Word displays dotted gridlines between cells. These help you to see which cell you are working in. These can be hidden, by, for instance, choosing **Table-Gridlines** and clicking on the menu entry **Gridlines**. It is usually best to work with the gridlines on. Gridlines will not be printed. If you require borders, see Activity 4.5.

exercise 4.4

- ❏ Open a new document.
- ❏ Type in the heading below.
- ❏ Create a table either by using **Table-Insert Table** command or the **TABLE** button, with three columns and one row.
- ❏ Enter the text into the columns, moving between columns using the **TAB** button. Also use the **TAB** button to create each new row in the table. If you need to adjust the width of the columns do so by dragging the column boundary. Do not try to format the column headings yet.
- ❏ Save the document as **Fatlim** and close **Fatlim**.

How much fat is the limit?		
Type of fat	*Saturated*	*Other fats*
12.5st(80kg) man		
Inactive	28g	68g
Quite active	35g	82g
Very active	42g	97g
9.5st(61kg) woman		
Inactive	22g	51g
Quite active	27g	63g
Very active	31g	74g

activity 4.3 Improving Your Table

Selecting within a table

In order to edit, format or add a border to certain parts of a table it is necessary to select specific parts of the table. Remember that the selected area will be highlighted in black. Selection can be achieved as indicated:

Selecting components of a table

To select	Operation
cell	click in the cell's selection area, which is a strip down its left side where the mouse pointer changes to a right pointing arrow.
any rectangular area of cells	place the mouse pointer anywhere in the top left cell and drag down and to the right until the area you want is selected.
row	click in the row selection bar to the left of the row, or double click in any cell's selection area in the row. Alternatively choose **Table-Select Row.**
column	click in the column selection bar at the top of the column, or click anywhere in the column with the right mouse button. Alternatively choose **Table-Select Column**.
whole table	point to the leftmost column, hold down the right mouse button, and drag across the table. Alternatively, choose **Table-Select Table**.

Once you have selected text within a table it is possible to apply formatting, moving, copying and other operations to text in the same way as with text elsewhere in the document. For example, with appropriate cells selected:

Table Operations

To	Do this
delete	choose **Edit-Cut**
copy	choose **Edit-Copy** or **Edit-Cut**. Move the insertion point and choose **Edit-Paste**
display the headings in each column in bold	select the first row of the table, containing the headings and click on the **BOLD** button
align text within a cell	set tab stops
adjust the alignment of paragraphs	click **JUSTIFICATION FORMATTING** buttons
move a row of cells	select the row. Drag the selected rows to the new location. Position the mouse pointer at the beginning of the selected rows, then release the left mouse button.
sort a table on the basis of the contents in a given column	select the sort column. Choose **Table-Sort Text.** The **Sort Text** dilaog box will be displayed. Select **Sort by Paragraphs** and then, for Type choose **Text**. Click on **OK**. Rows are ordered alphabetically according to the text in the sorted column.

exercise 4.5

Open the document **Fatlim**. Format the column headings by first selecting them and then applying appropriate formatting as above.

❏ to select the first cell, click on its left side.

❏ click on the bold and italic buttons to format the text.

❏ repeat this operation with the other cells whose text requires formatting.

When finished **Fatlim** should appear as it does in this book. Save the file.

exercise 4.6

In a new document:

❏ insert a table with three columns and one row using **Table-Insert Table**

❏ adjust the column widths by dragging them to accommodate the following addresses.

❏ insert the addresses into the cells.

❏ sort the table on the basis of the name column contents, by selecting that column, and choosing **Table-Sort Text** and appropraite options from the **Sort Text** dialog box. Rows should be ordered alphabetically according to the text in the sorted column.

❐ to add a row for column headings place the pointer in the top left hand corner and use *Table – Insert Rows.*

❐ enter the text of the column headings.

❐ save the document as **Address.**

Supplier	Address	Telephone
Universal Gym (Europe) Ltd	Hutton, Brentwood, Essex, CM13 1XA	0277-221122
Atlanta Sports Industries Ltd	Atlanta House, Rotherway, Euroway Estate, Maltby, Rotherham, S66 8QN	0709-700555
Physique Training Equipment Ltd	Bankfield Mill, Greenfield Road, Colne, Lancashire, BB8 9PD.	0282-863300

Editing a table

As you develop a table you will find that you may need to insert or delete a row or column, delete or insert single cells, or split a table into two separate tables. This may be achieved by:

Table Editing Operations

Action	How
insert a row	select the row below where you want to insert a new row, and click the **Table** button on the toolbar, or choose *Table-Insert Rows*. To insert a new row at the bottom of the table place the cursor below the last row of the table and choose *Table-Insert Rows*, or alternatively press **TAB**.
insert a column	Select the column to the right of where you wish to add the new column and click the table icon on the toolbar or choose *Table-Insert Columns*. To enter a column to the right of the table, place the cursor to the right of the table and choose *Table-Insert Columns*.
delete a row	select the row or rows and choose *Table-Delete Rows*.
delete a column	select the column or columns and choose *Table -Delete Columns*.
insert a single cell	place the insertion point in a cell and choose *Table-Insert Cells*. Decide where to shift the displaced cells to i.e. either to the right on the row or down the column. Choose **Insert Entire Row or Column**, if you are accidentally using the wrong command!
delete a single cell	proceed as for inserting a single cell, choosing whether to close up the row or column.

split a table into two separate tables	select the row which is to become the top row of the second table and choose **Table-Split Table**. A normal paragraph will be inserted to break the table into two parts. This command offers the only way of inserting normal text above a table at the start of a document.

exercise 4.7

This exercise asks you to use some of the formatting skills that you have learnt in using tables to design a form. There are a number of tips for form design:

❑ Remember the forms purpose, and keep the gaps the right size.

❑ Leave bigger gaps for manual infilling

❑ Request all necessary information but no unnecessary information

❑ Ask for information in a logical sequence.

❑ The headings should be clear and designed to help the reader to understand the form.

Taking all of these points into consideration we wish to design a form for application of membership for a Health and Fitness Club, that looks something like the one shown below, but which may be formatted slightly differently if you choose. I have used borders to print the gridlines so that you can see where they are positioned. You do not need to do this. Proceed thus:

❑ type in the first three rows

❑ justify and format these three rows as you choose.

❑ insert a table with four columns using **Table-Insert Table**

❑ start to enter the labels. You may need to drag the column boundaries to a position so that the labels are displayed sensibly.

❑ to enter 'For Office Use Only' you will need to widen the first column on this row only.

❑ Select the appropriate cell.

❑ drag the column boundary to accommodate the text.

❑ when you have completed this first part of the table, move the cursor below the table, press **ENTER** to insert a row, and insert a further table with **Table-Insert Table**, immediately below the first table. This table should have six columns of approximately equal width. You may need to drag column widths to align the two tables. In addition you should delete any space between the two tables.

❑ Next enter the final text into this table.

❑ Format all of the labels by displaying them in bold.

❑ Save as **Appform**. We will return to this document later to improve it.

Chelmer Leisure and Recreation Centre
Health and Fitness Club

Membership Application Form

Name				
Address				
		Telephone		
Occupation		Date of Birth		
Sporting Interests		Date of Joining		
For Office Use Only				
Date Subs Due		Subs Paid	Mem.Cat	

Table formatting

The table formatting command *Table-Cell Height and Width* allow you to format your table.

The Column sub-dialog box allows you to specify: width of columns, and

space between columns, for each column in turn.

The Row sub-dialog box covers many aspects of table formatting including:

indent from left	moves the whole table or selection to the right to leave an indent space at the left
height of rows m-n	normally set to **Auto**, which gives a row height sufficient for the highest cell. This can instead be specified
alignment	can be set to Left, Centre, or Right to align selected rows or the whole table.

These commands, together with other formatting that is available for all text offer a wide range of formatting options. To view the effect of formatting on the table, do not forget to view your document in Page Layout View.

exercise 4.8

❏ View **Appform** in Page Layout View.

❏ Select the table.

❏ Using *Table-Cell Height and Width* and the Column sub-dialog box change the space between columns to 0.5 cm.

❏ Select the whole table, and using *Table-Cell Height and Width* and the Row sub-dialog box and Alignment centre the table on the page. Save the document as **Appform**.

activity 4.4 Putting existing text into a table

If you already have a table laid out using tab characters, or some columns of text separated by commas, this can be converted into a table by:

❑ selecting the original table

❑ choosing **Table-Convert Text to Table**.

Word will examine the existing text and convert it to a table with suitable column widths. If Word can not determine how to convert the text, it displays a dialog box listing different conversion options.

If the resultant table is not as you would like it remember to use **Edit-Undo** before taking any other action.

Alternatively a table may be converted into regular text paragraphs. Simply select the rows of the table to be converted to text, and choose **Table-Convert Table to Text**. Select an appropriate **Separate Text With** option and choose **OK**.

exercise 4.9

❑ Open the document **Times.** This has existing tab stops.

❑ Select the section showing opening times.

❑ Choose **Table-Convert Text to Table**. The text should appear as a table with the gridlines displayed.

❑ You may need to drag the column boundaries so that the text is all displayed in the most effective way.

❑ Save the document as **Times1**

exercise 4.10

We now want to start to design a simple questionnaire and to be a little more ambitious in our use of tables. This is the questionnaire that we wish to start to design: I have printed borders so that you can see where the gridlines are, but you do not need to do this yet.

Chelmer Leisure and Recreation Centre
Health and Fitness Club

Market Research Questionnaire

Occupation		Sex(M/F)		
Age Band		**Smoking**		
Under 20		Non-smoker		
21-30		Pipe and/or cigar		
31-40		Under 10 cigs a day		
41-50		20 cigs a day		
51-60		30 cigs a day		
Over 60				
Which of the following would you be interested in attending? (Please Tick)		*Not at all*	*Somewhat*	*Very much*
Workshops on:				
Diet/Nutrition				
Stress Management				
Exercise				
Health Screening:				
Coronary Risk Assessment				
Cholesterol Check				
Blood Pressure Check				
Flexibility				
Strength				
Dietary Analysis				
Aerobic Fitness				

Please return this questionnaire to Chelmer Leisure and Recreation Centre.
Thank you for your co-operation.

- ❏ Open a new document.
- ❏ Type in the title and format and centre it.
- ❏ Place the insertion point on a new line and choose *Table-Insert Table*, and create a table with four columns.
- ❏ Enter the text in the table down to 'Over 60', using the **TAB** key to move between cells.
- ❏ Press the **TAB** key a few times to create a few empty cells. Leave one blank row and then
- ❏ Select these empty cells and drag the column boundaries on the bottom part of the table so that the cells will accommodate the text.
- ❏ Enter the text in the lower part of the table into the new cells.
- ❏ Format the text as appropriate
- ❏ Save the document as **Question**.

activity 4.5 Applying borders and shading to text

You will have observed that both the form designed in Exercise 4.7 and the questionnaire designed in Exercise 4.10 require additional formatting. This can be achieved by the use of borders and shading.

The design of a document can be improved significantly if borders, lines, and shading are used sparingly. Borders and shading can be applied to paragraphs of text, graphics or the cells in a table. With a colour printer, you can print coloured borders and shading. This activity introduces the basics of borders and shading and leaves you to experiment further with the immense potential of these features.

Quick Borders and Shading – Table Autoformat

A quick way to apply borders and shading to a table is to use *Table-Table Autoformat*, which displays the Table Autoformat dialog box. This dialog box lists a series of preset formats, and shows their format through a Preview box. These preset formats can be modified by changing: Borders, Shading, Font, Colour and AutoFit. It is also possible to apply Special formats to: Heading Rows, First Column, Last Row and Last Column.

exercise 4.11

❑   Open the document **Address**.

❑   Select the table

❑   Choose *Table-Table Autoformat*

❑   Experiment with the different standard formats, until the table resembles the table below.

Supplier	Address	Telephone
Universal Gym (Europe) Ltd	Hutton, Brentwood, Essex, CM13 1XA	0277-221122
Atlanta Sports Industries Ltd	Atlanta House, Rotherway Rotoway Estate, Maltby, Rotherham, S66 8QN	0709-700555
Physique Training Equipment Ltd	Bankfield Mill, Greenfield Road, Colne, Lancashire, BB8 9PD.	0282-863300

Applying and Formatting Borders

To **apply a border**, select the items to which a border is to be applied, then choose *Format-Borders and Shading*. This displays the **Paragraph Borders and Shading** dialog box. If no text is selected, but the insertion point is in normal text, the border is applied to the paragraph that contains the insertion point.

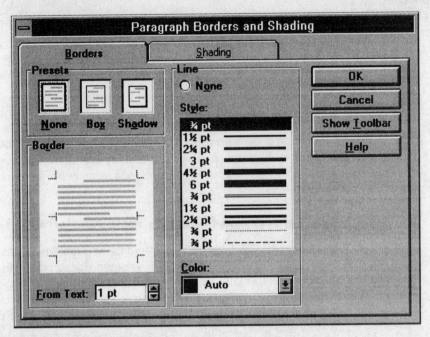

To **apply a box**, click on the box option under **Presets**, and then click a line style under **Line**. If you want to change the colour of the border, select a colour in the **Color** box.

To **create a custom border** or to add lines within a box, click the border sample where you want to apply a border, such as a horizontal line, and then click a line style under **Line**.

To **change the distance of the border from the text** click on an appropriate value in the **From Text** box. When you have finished selecting options, choose **OK**.

Removing and Changing Borders

To remove or change a border, first select the item that has the border to be removed or changed. Choose ***Format-Borders and Shading***. Then:

❏ to remove all borders, click **None** under **Presets**, or

❏ to remove one border at a time, click the border you want to remove on the border sample and then click **None** under **Line**.

Click on **OK**.

Borders may also be changed by selecting the item with the border to be changed. Choosing ***Format-Borders and Shading***, and changing the selected options in the **Borders** sub-dialog box.

exercise 4.12

This exercise encourages you to explore some of the basics of applying borders to text.

❏ Open the document **Openday**, that you created in Exercise 2.8.

❏ Select all of the text in this document.

❏ Choose *Format-Borders and Shading* to display the **Paragraph Borders and Shading** dialog box.

❏ Click on the **Box** option under **Presets**.

❏ Choose a line style e.g. double, under **Line**.

❏ Click on the **Shadow** box. Choose **OK**

❏ Examine, print and save your document as **Openday**.

exercise 4.13

This exercise attempts a more sophisticated use of borders in the use of border in applications based on tables such as an application form or questionnaire.

❏ Open the document **Appform**

❏ Create borders around the cells in which data is to be entered, by selecting each cell in turn and:

❏ Choose *Format-Borders and Shading*.

❏ Click on the **Box** option under **Presets**.

❏ Choose a line style under **Line**. Choose **OK**.

❏ Next select the row with 'For Office Use Only'.

❏ Choose *Format-Borders and Shading*.

❏ Click on the **None** option under **Presets**.

❏ Select the top border by clicking on this border on the sample.

❏ Select a double line under **Line**.

❏ Select the bottom row.

❏ Choose *Format-Borders and Shading*, and **Grid** under **Presets** and an appropriate line. Choose **OK**.

❏ Choose *Table-Gridlines* and turn off the gridlines so that you can view your formatting and borders.

Chelmer Leisure and Recreation Centre
Health and Fitness Club
Membership Application Form

Name	
Address	

		Telephone	
Occupation		Date of Birth	
Sporting Interests		Date of Joining	

For Office Use Only

Date Subs Due		Subs Paid		Mem.Cat	

Applying Shading

Shading can be applied to paragraphs or the cells in a table. If you have a colour printer, you can shade tables and paragraphs with colours.

Shading can be used to shade a short section in a newsletter, or an important column of figures in a table. Shading on paragraphs covers the text. Shading in table cells fills the cell.

Remember: Shading affects the legibility of the text. In general, light shading of 20 % or less is most effective. Small font sizes are difficult to read with shading. The use of bold may improve the text legibility.

The **Shading** sub-dialog box can be called by choosing *Format-Borders and Shading*, and clicking on the **Shading** title. The **Shading** sub-dialog box has the following options:

None	Removes the shading from selection
Custom	Allows you to create a customised shading
Shading	Displays percentages of grey shading from 5 to 90% as well as several patterns including clear and solid
Foreground	The default foreground dolour, Auto, is the colour used to display text on the screen i.e. usually black. 16 colours are available.
Background	The default background colour, Auto, is the colour that is used to display the background on the screen, i.e. usually white. 16 colours are available.

Shading can be applied by selecting an appropriate Shading, Pattern, Foreground and Background Colour, and choosing **OK** to close the **Shading** sub-dialog box.

exercise 4.14

We wish to improve the questionnaire that we started to design earlier and to add borders and shading. This is a relatively ambitious project and although the basic steps are outlined below you are likely to find that parts of tables have moved to places where you do not want them. You need to be confident in working with tables to succeed with this exercise!

Chelmer Leisure and Recreation Centre Market Research Questionnaire		

Occupation		Sex(M/F)	

Age Band		Smoking	
Under 20		Non-smoker	
21-30		Pipe and/or cigar	
31-40		Under 10 cigs a day	
41-50		20 cigs a day	
51-60		30 cigs a day	
Over 60			

Which of the following would you be interested in attending?(Please Tick)	Not at all	Somewhat	Very much
Workshops on:			
Diet/Nutrition			
Stress Management			
Exercise			
Health Screening:			
Coronary Risk Assessment			
Cholesterol Check			
Blood Pressure Check			
Flexibility			
Strength			
Dietary Analysis			
Aerobic Fitness			

Please return this questionnaire to Chelmer Leisure and Recreation Centre. Thank you for your co-operation.

To add borders and shading to the questionnaire:

Select the first two lines i.e. the heading.

Choose *Format-Borders and Shading* and then in the **Paragraph Borders and Shading** dialog box choose **Box**, **Shadow** and an appropriate double line.

Next select each set of boxes with labels and associated reply boxes and apply a single line border with the Grid.

The top two sets of boxes would look better if they were separated. Select the top part of the third column and insert a column using *Table-Insert Cells*, and choosing **Shift Cells Right**.

With the top part of the table selected move the column boundary to make this new column fairly narrow.

Select the new column and remove any borders. In so doing you may manage to remove some of the borders that you have just created. Just insert them again. It's all good practice.

Now apply shading to each of the cells shown as shaded in the example above. To do this

Select the cell, and choose *Format-Borders and Shading* and then click on the Shading heading. This displays the **Shading** sub-dialog box.

Click on **Custom**, Choose a **Shading**, say **20%**. Select colours using **Foreground** and **Background** if you have a colour printer!

Save your document as **Question** and print it.

Special Tips for Borders and Shading

The ways in which you can apply borders and shading are almost endless. Here are just a few ideas that might be useful:

1. Word applies borders to the edges of a selected graphic. If you have **cropped close to the image and need to add space** between the image and the border, select the graphic to display the sizing handles. Press **SHIFT** and drag the centre handles on each side of the graphic to increase the space between the edge of the graphic and the image.

2. To **place graphics adjacent to one another** place the graphics in a table, and then apply borders to the table cells.

3. To **add a double border to separate column headings from table entries** first apply single borders on all sides of the cell. First select the table, then choose *Format-Borders and Shading* and under **Presets** select **Grid**, then **OK**. Then select the first row of the table and change the line style of the border below the row.

4. You can **apply borders to paragraphs and graphics within a table cell** in addition to the borders that you apply to the cell itself.

5. If you want to **apply the same border to a group of paragraphs**, all paragraphs must have the same indents. Otherwise paragraphs are placed in separate boxes. To place all text in one box, convert the text to a one column table.

integrative exercises

exercise 4.15

In this exercise we wish to create the following table which summarises a timetable for activities at the Centre during the week.

❑ Open a new document.

❑ Enter the heading, and format and centre the text.

❑ Choose **Table-Insert Table**. Create a table with six columns.

❑ Enter the text into the table.

❑ Select the table, and apply borders using **Format-Borders and Shading**. Apply a Grid.

❑ Select appropriate cells and apply Shading using **Format-Borders and Shading.**

❑ Save the document as **Timetble.**

Chelmer Leisure and Recreation Centre

ACTIVITY PROGRAMME

FITNESS SUITE	Monday	Tuesday	Wednesday	Thursday	Friday
Daytime					
10.00 – 11.00am	Ladies Aerobics	Mens Multi-gym	Ladies Aerobics		Body Conditioning
11.00 – 12.00pm	Weight Training			Weight Training	Step Aerobics
2.00 - 3.00pm		Ladies Multi-gym	Body Conditioning	Step Aerobics	Mens Multi-gym
3.00 – 4.00pm	Body conditioning		Weight Training	Multi-gym	
Evening					
7.00 – 9.00pm	Step Aerobics	Family Multi-gym	Weight Training	Body Conditioning	

exercise 4.16

The following document uses a table to set up a simple questionnaire. It is printed in two formats below, one which shows the completed questionnaire and another that demonstrates the way in which a table has been used to create the questionnaire. You should now be able to set up an appropriate table, apply borders and enter the text without any additional instructions

Chelmer Leisure and Recreation Centre
Staff Workshops in IT

It is planned to run some staff development workshops in IT, during a week in the near future. If you are interested in attending sessions please indicate your area of interest in the following questionnaire.

These sessions could be run in two forms

1. General introduction to software, to introduce IT skills.

2. A more user oriented approach aimed primarily at experimenting with your ideas and to judge how to make use of the facilities available to you.

Please return completed forms to the IT Co-ordinator.

Name:

Please tick those areas of interest.

Introducing IT skills

Introducing Windows 3.1 □

Introduction to Word Processing using Microsoft Word for Windows □

Introduction to Graphics using Microsoft Word for Windows □

Introduction to Spreadsheets using Microsoft Excel □

Introduction to Databases using dBaseIV □

Using IT in your area of work.

Word Processing □

Spreadsheets □

Graphics □

Please indicate below if you feel that there are any other areas of IT you wish to investigate:

The version below shows how the table is used in the design of the questionnaire:

Chelmer Leisure and Recreation Centre
Staff Workshops in IT

It is planned to run some staff development workshops in IT, during a week in the near future. If you are interested in attending sessions please indicate your area of interest in the following questionnaire.

These sessions could be run in two forms

1. General introduction to software, to introduce IT skills.

2. A more user oriented approach aimed primarily at experimenting with your ideas and to judge how to make use of the facilities available to you.

Please return completed forms to the IT Co-ordinator.

Name:

Please tick those areas of interest.

Introducing IT skills

Introducing Windows 3.1	
Introduction to Word Processing using Microsoft Word for Windows	
Introduction to Graphics using Microsoft Word for Windows	
Introduction to Spreadsheets using Microsoft Excel	
Introduction to Databases using dBaseIV	

Using IT in your area of work.

Word Processing	
Spreadsheets	
Graphics	

Please indicate below if you feel that there are any other areas of IT you wish to investigate:

activity 4.6 Tabs in tables

Text may be entered into a table and it can be formatted in the same way as text which is not in a table. Most alignment that is needed in tables can be achieved by aligning text within the column, for example, a column may be centred or if it contains figures, right aligned.

Other formatting may be used such as setting margins or tabs. However, in tables the TAB key has the effect of moving the insertion point to the next cell in the table, not inserting a tab character as would happen in normal text. Tab characters may be inserted into table cells by pressing the **CTRL** and **TAB** keys together.

exercise 4.15 Setting and using tabs in a table

The aim of this exercise is to explore tabs within tables by creating the summary statistics table shown on the next page.

☐ Enter the heading and under it insert a table with four columns and three rows.

☐ Enter the text in the first row and column and adjust the width of the first column.

☐ Select decimal tab by clicking on the symbol at the left of the ruler until the decimal tab character is displayed.

☐ Select the six empty cells in the table (rightmost 3 columns and lower 2 rows). Click on the ruler of column 2 to set a decimal tab. Position it slightly to the right of the column. Now if you click on any of the six cells you should see a decimal tab in the ruler for the selected cell.

☐ Enter the data shown. You will find that the insertion point will be ready positioned on the tab as you move to each cell.

Note: inserting a single decimal tab on the ruler within a cell has the effect of automatically aligning the text on the decimal point without having to use **CTRL+TAB** to position the text under the tab. When using any other tabs – left, centre, right – or using more than one tab, **CTRL+TAB** needs to be used.

☐ Now select a left, tab, place the insertion point in the top of column 2 (i.e. the cell containing the text Court 1) and set a left tab on the ruler for the selected cell.

☐ Position the insertion point before the C of Court and press **CTRL+TAB**. The text should move to the tab position set. You may wish to experiment with different tab types for the other two headings.

Note: Tabs set in tables may be edited using **Format-Tabs** as previously described.

Squash court average daily use for January 1995

	Court 1	Court 2	Court 3
Average number of bookings	11.4	10.8	11.1
Standard deviation	2.45	2.13	2.67

Session 5
Large Documents

objectives

In this session the activities concentrate on word processing features that are applicable to documents of more than one page. If the work being produced is for assessment it is often in the form of a report and may be several pages long. Features covered are:

- ☐ controlling page breaks
- ☐ numbering pages
- ☐ adding headers and footers
- ☐ styles
- ☐ sections
- ☐ contents and index

For most long documents it is useful to know how to add headers and footers, page numbers and to be able to control page breaks. If you produce a number of long documents then you are likely to develop a personal style for the text and headings. This style can be recorded as a style template for use with subsequent documents.

activity 5.1 Combining smaller documents into a larger one

You may be working on a report and have information in several files. These files can be combined into one file so that, for example, appropriate headers and footers and page numbers may be added. In the following example a large document will be created from smaller documents created in previous exercises.

exercise 5.1

Documents needed for this exercise are **Front, Termref, Centre, Usage, Question, Findings** and **Summary**.

- ☐ Open the document file **Front** and using *File-Save As* save this as **Report**.
- ☐ Use **CTRL+END** to move to the end of the document and press **ENTER** to make a new line.
- ☐ Choose *Insert-File* and the **File** dialog box appears.
- ☐ From the list of files select the file **Termref** and click on **OK**.

❏ Move to the end of the document.

❏ Repeat the last three steps to insert each of the document files **Centre, Usage, Question, Findings** and **Summary**.

❏ Save this file using *File-Save.*

activity 5.2 Pagination and Page Numbering

As the document being created gets larger Word automatically inserts a page break at the end of each page. Automatic page breaks are called *soft* breaks and are shown in normal view as a dotted line. As the document is edited and revised Word re-positions the page breaks accordingly. This is known as re-pagination. Re-pagination occurs whenever you pause during keying. To alter the way in which page breaks occur then manual or *hard* breaks can be inserted.

Adding or removing page breaks

To add a page break

❏ first position the insertion point at the place where the page break is to occur and

either

❏ use *Insert-Break* and select **Page Break** from the **Break** dialog box.

or

❏ the keyboard shortcut is to press **CTRL+ENTER** simultaneously.

In normal view a dotted line appears at the point of the *hard* page break. In a *hard* break the words Page Break appear in the middle of the line.

A *hard* page break may be selected in the same way as a line of text can be selected i.e. by positioning the mouse pointer in the left edge of the screen, level with the page break and clicking. Once selected the page break can be removed. It is not possible to remove *soft* page breaks, these can be controlled either by inserting *hard* page breaks or with paragraph formatting. If possible it is best to avoid *hard* page breaks in a long document as they need to be revised manually whenever the document is revised.

exercise 5.2

Recall the file **Report** created in the last exercise to insert appropriate page breaks.

❏ Position the cursor at the end of the titles and press **CTRL+ENTER.** This should insert a *hard* break at the end of the title page. The body of the report should start on the next page.

❏ Repeat this process to put a page break before each heading. You may try adjusting the spacing on the title page to spread out the titles.

❏ Use *File-Print Preview* to see how the document looks. Save this document as **Report**.

❏ For use in the following exercises make two copies of this document. Use *File-Save As* and save one as **Report1**, repeat and save the second copy as **Report2**. Close all documents.

Page numbering

There are two methods of inserting page numbers:

1. Using *Insert-Page Numbers.* Page numbers may be inserted using *Insert-Page Numbers*. Page numbers may be placed at the bottom of the page (footer) or at the top of the page (header). The alignment of the number can be chosen and whether or not all pages are to be numbered except the first. Remove the x from the **Show Number on First Page** to omit the number from the first page, this is useful for documents that have a title page as the first page.

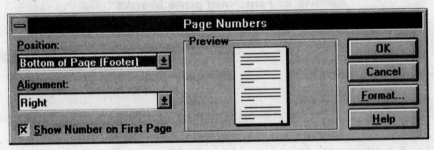

2. As part of a header or footer. This is discussed in the next section.

exercise 5.3

Apply page numbering to the document **Report1**:

❏ Use *Insert-Page Numbers* to add page numbers to the document.

❏ Check that **Position: Bottom of Page (Footer)** and **Alignment: Centre** are selected.

❏ Click on the **Format** button and choose numbering to **Start At** 0. This is so that the second page will have a page number of 1.

❏ Click on **OK**.

❏ Choose *View-Page Layout*. In **Page Layout** view the page numbers should be visible at the bottom of each page.

❏ Use *File-Print Preview* to see the effect.

❏ Save the document **Report1**.

If the page numbers are not visible when the document is previewed, then their position in the bottom margin may need adjusting. To do this choose *File-Page Setup* and increase the distance of the header or footer from the edge. You may also need to adjust the position of the top and bottom margins to accommodate the change.

Printing specified pages

In the **Print** dialog box click on the **Pages** option button. In the associated text box list the page numbers to be printed. For example, to print pages 5, 7, and 9 simply type 5,7,9, to print pages 5 to 8 inclusive type 5-8.

activity 5.3 Headers and Footers

A header is text or graphics that appears at the top of every page. A footer appears at the bottom of every page. They are useful in long documents as they can be used to indicate, for example, the chapter or section title. In business documents they may contain a reference number or company logo. If the work is an assignment a header or footer could be used to put the author's name on each page. Word prints headers in the top margin and footers in the bottom margin.

As well as being able to add headers and footers that are the same on every page Word also offers choices of customising headers and footers, these are:

❏ if the document is to be printed on both sides of the paper then headers and footers can be set up so that even numbered pages have one header and odd numbered pages have a different one.

❏ if the first page of the document is different from the rest of the document, for example, it is a title page, then headers and footers can be set so that they different on the first page.

if the document is divided into sections then different headers and footers can be applied to each section. Sections are discussed in Activity 5.6.

Adding or removing a header or footer

To add a header or a footer to your document, use ***View-Header and Footer*** and the document switches to a page layout view with the text of each page shown in grey (or lighter than normal). and a **Header and Footer** tool bar appears.

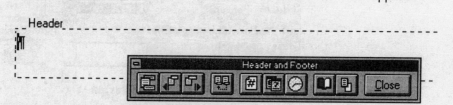

Headers and footers have pre-set tabs, there is a centre tab in the middle of the page and a right tab at the right edge of the page. By using the pre-set tabs then the headers or footers will be consistent through the document. Choose the font and tab across to the position required and type in the text for the header or footer. Using the buttons, as described following, enter text for headers and footers as required and when finished click on **Close**.

Icons and buttons in the Header/Footer Pane bar

The first button on the header and footer tool bar allows you to switch between the header and footer. The second two buttons allow forward and backward movement between different headers or footers. There will only be different headers and footers, if Different First Page, or Different Odd and Even Pages, in Page Setup have been selected or there are different sections in the document. The next button is the **Same as Previous** button. Click on the **Same as Previous** button if the header or footer is to be different from the header or footer in the previous section. Activity 5.6 discusses dividing the document up into sections.

There are three buttons in the centre of the header and footer tool bar these are (working from left to right):

❑ page numbering

❑ date

❑ time

To put the date, the time or the page number into a header or footer, position the insertion point and then click on the appropriate icon.

The next two buttons are **Page Setup** and **Show/Hide Text**. Clicking on **Page Setup** will display the Page Setup dialog box. Clicking on **Show/Hide Text** will toggle between showing or hiding the document text.

When the text for the header or footer has been typed in click on the **Close** button to close the pane.

Before printing it is a good idea to preview the document, headers and footers can be positioned by choosing *File-Page Setup* and defining their required position in the **From Edge** section of the **Page Setup-Margins** dialog box.

Page Numbering in Headers or Footers

Through the *Insert-Page Numbers* command page numbering can be controlled. Click on the **Format** button to display the **Page Number Format** dialog box:

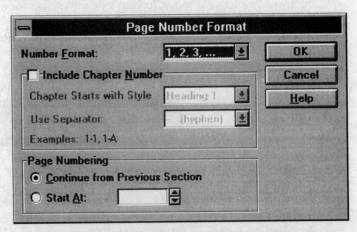

The format of page numbering may be chosen from the **Number Format** box, i.e. Arabic or Roman numerals or alphabetic numbering. This can be done by opening the **Number Format** list box. It is also possible to alter the number at which page numbering starts. This can be useful if the document is long and is stored as separate files. The start page number of the second and subsequent files may be altered accordingly. Different formats of page numbering may be used in different sections of a document.

Editing or Removing existing Headers and Footers

To remove or edit an existing header or footer:

❑ Use *View-Header and Footer* and display either the Header or Footer using the **Switch between Header and Footer** button.

❑ Edit the text in the header or footer in the normal fashion. Text may be pasted into the header or footer, or copied from it. To remove the header/footer simply delete all the text.

❑ Click on **Close**.

exercise 5.4

In this exercise a header and a footer are added to the document **Qdesign**. Open the document.

❑ Choose *View-Header and Footer* and the insertion point is ready positioned in the header.

❑ Press the **TAB** key to move to the centre tab and type in the text **Adjusting Margins.**

❑ Click on the **Switch between Header and Footer** button to display the footer.

❑ Press the **TAB** key twice to move to the right tab and type in your name.

❑ Click on **Close**.

❑ Preview the document and make any adjustments to the positions of the header and footer as described above. Also view the document with page layout view to see the header and footer. Save the document as **Qdesign** and print it.

❑ From normal view use *View-Header and Footer* and display the footer.

❑ Select the footer text and delete it.

❑ Click on **Close**. Preview the document or use page layout view to see the effect but it is not necessary to save this change.

Headers and footers that are different on the first page

To select this option:

❑ Choose *View-Header and Footer* and click on the **Page Setup** button.

---

[1] A number is commonly used for a reference mark.

❏ Click in the **Different First Page** check box. This will create a **First Header** and a **First Footer** as well as the normal **Header** and **Footer**. The text in a First Header may be different from the Header and the text in a First Footer may be different from the Footer.

❏ Use the **Switch between Header and Footer** button and the **Show Next** and the **Show Previous** buttons to navigate to the header or footer desired and key in the text.

❏ Click on **Close**.

exercise 5.5

Using the document **Report2** this exercise adds a header and a footer both of which will not appear on the first page of the document. Page numbering is incorporated into the footer.

❏ Choose *View-Header and Footer*.

❏ Use the **Page Number Format** dialog box to start the page numbering at 0 so that the first page of text will appear to be page 1.

❏ Click on the **Page** Setup button and click in the **Different First Page** check box.

❏ Move to the header (use the **Show Next** button to move to header from first header).

❏ Key in the text 'Fitness Suite Feasibility Study'.

❏ Move to the footer (not the first footer).

❏ Press the **TAB** key once and click on the page numbering icon.

❏ Press **TAB** again and key in your name.

❏ Click on **Close**.

❏ Save the document **Report2**.

At this point review and compare both the documents **Report1** and **Report2**. If you wish, make extra copies of the document **Report** and experiment with headers and footers.

Odd and even headers and footers

Odd and even headers and footers are used when the finished document will be printed like a book where both sides of the paper are printed on. In a book left hand pages are even numbered and right hand pages are odd numbered. A header or footer can be defined so that it reads across from an even to an odd page. Different information about the document can appear on odd and even pages, for example, chapter title on even pages and section title on odd pages. To achieve this:

❏ Choose *View-Header and Footer* and click on the **Page Setup** button.

❏ Click on the **Different Odd and Even Pages** check box. This will create an **Even Header,** an **Odd Header,** an **Even Footer,** and an **Odd Footer**. The text in the Even Header may be different from the Odd Header and the text in a Even Footer may be different from the Odd Footer.

❏ Use the **Switch between Header and Footer** button and the **Show Next** and the **Show Previous** buttons to navigate to the header or footer desired and key in the text.

❏ Click on **Close**.

Note that the odd and even headers/footers option may be used in conjunction with the different first page option.

Footnotes and Endnotes

Footnotes and endnotes are notes of reference, explanation, or comment. A word in the main text can be marked with a footnote or endnote reference mark[1]. Footnotes are found at the bottom of the page and endnotes are found at the end of the document. Word allows footnotes and endnotes of any length to be added to a document.

Text used in a footnote can be formatted just as any other text. To add a footnote or endnote:

❏ First position the insertion point at the end of the word that the footnote or endnote is to refer to.

❏ Use *Insert-Footnote* and the **Footnote and Endnote** dialog box appears:

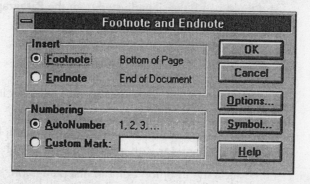

❏ Click on **OK** and a footnote pane appears as shown below. A reference mark is positioned in the document at the position of the insertion point.

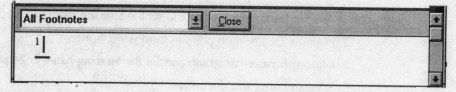

❏ Key in the text. The insertion point is ready positioned following the reference mark.

❏ Click on **Close**.

As footnotes or endnotes are added Word automatically numbers them. Word will automatically renumber footnote/endnote and reference marks whenever footnotes/endnotes are added, deleted, or moved.

activity 5.4 Paragraph Formatting

In session 3 formatting that can be applied to paragraphs has been investigated. In this session formatting that can be applied when creating a long document will be considered. By altering paragraph formatting the position of page breaks can be controlled.

Controlling amount of space between paragraphs

In many documents paragraphs have space between them. This book is an example. Instead of pressing **ENTER** to create a blank line between paragraphs Word allows you to define the amount of space before and after a paragraph. Use *Format-Paragraph* to display the Paragraph dialog box and in the spacing section the values in the **Before** and **After** boxes can be adjusted. Spacing is altered in increments of 6 points which is half a line. Note that if you have space after a paragraph and the following paragraph has space before it then the space between the paragraphs will be the sum of the before and after spacing.

Other paragraphs may require different spacing, for example headings or tables and these can be easily adjusted from the **Paragraph** dialog box.

exercise 5.6

This exercise experiments with altering the spacing between paragraphs. Open the document **Qdesign:**

- ☐ If you have a blank line in between paragraphs, remove them, click on the **Special Character** icon to show the paragraph marks.
- ☐ Position the insertion point in first paragraph.
- ☐ Choose *Format-Paragraph* and set the **Spacing Before** to 12 points (one line).
- ☐ Position the insertion point in second paragraph.
- ☐ Choose *Format-Paragraph* and set the **Spacing Before** to 24 points (two lines).
- ☐ Position the insertion point in third paragraph.
- ☐ Choose *Format-Paragraph* and set the **Spacing After** to 24 points (two lines).
- ☐ Save and print this document.
- ☐ Experiment with setting the line spacing before and after the paragraphs in this document.

Controlling page breaks using paragraph formatting

This is controlled through the pagination section of the **Format Paragraph-Text Flow** dialog box. There are three types of formatting available:

```
┌─ Pagination ──────────────────────────────────────┐
│ [X] Widow/Orphan Control      [ ] Keep with Next   │
│ [X] Keep Lines Together       [ ] Page Break Before │
└───────────────────────────────────────────────────┘
```

❏ **Keep Lines Together:** use this to prevent a page break within a paragraph. Word normally exercises Widow and Orphan control, if the **Widow/Orphan Control** box is checked, that is to say that it will prevent Widows and Orphans from occurring. A Widow is a single line at the beginning of a paragraph left at the bottom of a page and an Orphan is a single line at the end of a paragraph at the top of a page.

❏ **Keep with Next:** use this to prevent a page break occurring between the paragraph and the following one. For example, to keep a sub-heading with its following paragraph or to keep the lines of a table together.

❏ **Page Break Before:** if a paragraph such as a heading is formatted with **Page Break Before** then a page break will be inserted before the paragraph. If each chapter of your document is to appear on a new page then format the chapter heading with **Page Break Before** by clicking in the appropriate check box. To remove this page break the formatting must be removed from the paragraph.

By making use of these formatting options the need for *hard* pages breaks to be inserted in a long document can be eliminated. When the document is altered the page breaks will follow the rules applied in the paragraph formatting and consequently should occur in sensible places.

exercise 5.7

The *hard* breaks originally put into the document **Report** are to be replaced by *soft* breaks controlled by the type of paragraph formatting. Open the document **Report:**

❏ Remove the *hard* page break at the end of the title page by selecting it and pressing the **DELETE** key.

❏ Position the insertion point in the heading 'Terms of Reference'.

❏ Use *Format-Paragraph* and click on the **Page Break Before** check box. Click on **OK**. In normal view you should see a *soft* break inserted. Switch to page layout view or use *File-Print Preview* to verify the effect.

❏ Replace all the remaining *hard* breaks with *soft* breaks. Remove each one and format the heading paragraph using **Page Break Before.**

❏ Save the document **Report**.

activity 5.5 Using styles

A style is the name applied to the 'look' of the text in a document. The 'look' of the text depends upon the formatting instructions that have been applied to it. A heading is usually made to look different from the body of the text, i.e. it has a different style. In a document there may be different levels of headings, for example chapter or section headings and within these are sub-headings. Word has the facility for different styles to be created and stored under different names. Different styles can be used for different headings.

Various formatting may be applied to create a style

1. Character formatting such as
    - ☐ typeface
    - ☐ size
    - ☐ bold, italics or underlining.

2. Paragraph formatting such as
    - ☐ alignment
    - ☐ spacing
    - ☐ margins
    - ☐ pagination

3. Layout formatting such as
    - ☐ tabs
    - ☐ borders and shading.

4. Language formatting, if text is written in a different language then Word will know to use the appropriate dictionary (if available) when spell checking.

Selecting a style

Word comes with some pre-defined styles and these can be listed by opening the style list box at the leftmost end of the **Formatting** toolbar.

To select a style:

☐ position the insertion point, either to key in some new text or in an existing paragraph. If you wish to alter the style of a portion of the document which is more than one paragraph long, then select the required portion.

❏ open the **Style** list box and highlight the required style.

❏ either key in text which will have the selected style, or the chosen paragraph or portion will be changed into the new style.

To see definition of a style position the insertion point in some text that uses the style, say Normal, and choose *Format-Style.* In the **Style** dialog box a description of the style is given.

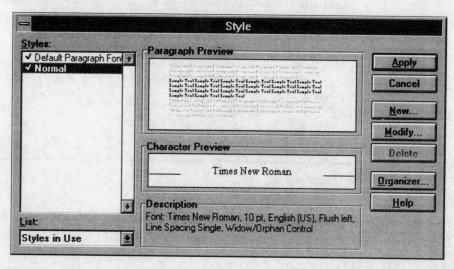

Styles may be used as the document is being keyed in or they can be applied after the text has been keyed in. The real advantage in using styles is in being able to define custom styles. Should an alteration in the style be desirable then by changing the definition of the style, all parts of the document that use that style will be altered accordingly. This makes it easier to produce consistent documents.

Defining a custom style

There are a number of ways in which a style can be defined, however, only one will be described, that is using the menu. Consider defining the style for the main body of the text in the document.

❏ Position the insertion point in a paragraph that is to take the main body style, or position it on a new line.

❏ Use *Format-Style* to display the **Style** dialog box.

❏ Click on the **New** button and in the **Name** box type in the name for the new style, e.g. **Text body.**

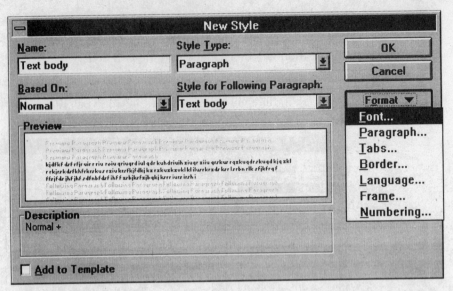

❏ Select the appropriate formatting by clicking on the **Format** button and of choosing from the list:

1. **Font** – produces **Font** dialog box.

2. **Paragraph** – produces **Format Paragraph** dialog box.

3. **Tabs** – produces **Tabs** dialog box.

4. **Border** – produces **Paragraph Borders and Shading** dialog box.

5. **Language** – produces **Language** dialog box.

6. **Frame** – produces **Frame** dialog box.

7. **Numbering** – produces **Bullets and Numbering** dialog box.

❏ Make required choices from these dialog boxes and click on **OK**.

❏ Choose the **Style For Following Paragraph** from the list box. In this case it would be **Text body.**

❏ When the style is defined click on **Apply.** The defined style name will be available through the style list box.

At the top of the dialog box there are two list boxes, a **Based On** box and a **Style For Following Paragraph** box. By basing your custom styles on one particular style formatting changes can be made easier. If all the styles are based on a style that has a Times New Roman font and a decision is made to change to Arial then by altering the font upon which the others are all based will cause them to be altered unless they have specific character formatting applied.

The **Style For Following Paragraph** list box defines the style that is to follow the one being used. The next paragraph will take on the style of the 'next style'. For the **Text body** style the next style should be **Text body** as the most likely paragraph to follow a paragraph written using the text body format is another paragraph using the same format. If the style is a heading style e.g. **Heading 1** then it is most likely that a text body paragraph will follow so for Heading 1 the next style should be **Text body**.

Note that heading styles (there are 8, Heading 1 to Heading 8) should only be used for headings. If a table of contents is required Word uses headings to generate it.

It is worth the extra effort in designing various styles to give your work a professional look. Do not use lots of different fonts, the best effects are achieved with one font used in different sizes with a variety of typefonts.

exercise 5.8

For this exercise open the document file **Front**. Formatting that has been previously set up can be defined as a style. Four styles are to be defined for this title page:

❏ First position the insertion point in the first line of the title page.

❏ Use *Format-Style*, click on **New** and in the **Name** box type in the name **Title1.**

❏ Click on the **Apply** button.

❏ Select the second line of the institution, open the style list box and select **Title1**. Nothing appears to happen except that the style of Title1 has been applied to that paragraph.

❏ Position the insertion point in the author name. As above create a style called **Title4**.

❏ Apply this style to the last four lines of the page. You may need to click on the **Format** button in the **Style** dialog box and choose **Paragraph** to remove spacing before/after a paragraph.

❏ In a similar manner define and apply suitable styles, **Title2** and **Title3** to the second and third portions of the page. Hint: keep paragraph spacing to zero, add spacing to the first line of a portion after the styles have been defined.

❏ Save the document as **Front**.

Modifying a style

You may change your mind about the styles which you have chosen and wish to make changes.

exercise 5.9

Using the document file **Front** make changes to the styles created in exercise 5.8.

❏ Position insertion point in text which has the style **Title1** applied to it.

❏ Choose *Format-Style* and click on **Modify**. Click on **Format**, choose **Font** and select a different font. Click on **OK**.

❏ Click on **OK** in the **Modify Style** dialog box and click on **Apply.** All text throughout the document defined with this style will take on these new properties.

❏ Experiment with the other styles. Changes to their fonts, sizes, margins and alignment can be made. If you prefer the styles you have chosen save the document.

Storing Styles in Templates

In session 3 the idea of using a template using 'boilerplate' or standard text was introduced. The flexibility of templates can be further increased by defining a set of styles that can be stored with a template. In fact it is possible to have a template without any text. The default template of NORMAL is an example, it contains Word's standard styles.

exercise 5.10

The two styles defined for the title page could also be used for title pages of other pieces of work. These styles can be saved as a template which can be applied to future documents. This exercise uses a straightforward method for setting up a style template.

❏ Open a new document using *File-New.*

❏ Select the **Template** option button.

❏ Choose Normal from the list of templates as the new template is to be based on this template. Click on **OK.**

❏ Type the word Title1 with your preferred formatting and set up the style **Title1** as described in Exercise 5.8.

❏ Repeat for each style i.e. on the next line type Title2 and set up the style **Title2** etc.

❏ Use *File-Save As* and type **Titles** in the file name box. This file is saved as a .dot template file. Close the file using *File-Close.*

To use this template, start a new document using *File-New* and select **Titles** from the list of templates. Replace the words Title1, Title2, Title3 and Title4 with the desired titles. It is not necessary to use all the styles each time a front page is created. Save the new title page in the usual manner.

You can combine text and style in a template, for example, the name of the institution could be used instead of Title1. You could remove the text in the template before saving i.e. before the last step above, to leave just the style definitions in the template.

Adding styles to a template

As a document is created styles may be defined which would be useful to be stored. These may be added to the document template by clicking in the **Add to Template** check box in the bottom left hand corner of the **Style** dialog box. When you save your document Word will ask if you wish to save the changes to the template.

Copying Styles

If you wish new styles to be added to the template file, or copied from one document to another, then this can be done using the **Organizer** dialog box. In the list on the left of the dialog box the styles used in the active document or its template are shown. Styles used in the Normal document template are listed on the right.

If you wish to use styles which have been stored in a template or document which is different from the template currently being used, then the styles from that template can be copied into the current document. This can be achieved using the **Organizer** dialog box and is illustrated in the following exercise.

exercise 5.11

In this exercise the styles created and saved in the template **Titles.dot** are to be merged into the document **Report**.

❐ Open the document file **Report.**

❐ Use *Format-Style* and click on **Organizer.**

❐ Click on **Close File** on the right side of the dialog box: Next click on **Open File** and select the template **Titles.dot**.

Note: You may select either a document or a template from which to copy styles. The **Open** dialog box allows you to change drive or directory; or to list document or template files.

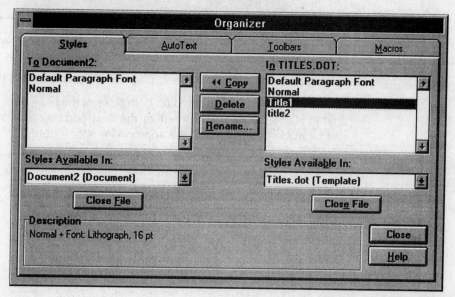

❐ Select **Title1** from the list of style names and click on ◄◄**Copy**. Repeat for other styles in this document which you may wish to copy.

❐ Click on **Close**.

❑ Open the Style list box (on the formatting toolbar) and you should be able to find the styles that you have copied will be listed.

❑ Apply these to the title page. Select each portion of the title page in turn and open the style list box and choose the appropriate style.

❑ Save the document **Report**.

activity 5.6 Dividing the document into sections

By dividing a document up into sections, different formatting such as different headers and footers, page numbering and orientation or layout can be achieved. A document can be divided into any number of sections and a section can be of any length. A section can be as short as one paragraph or as long as the whole document.

It is advisable to perform this activity when the text of the document is complete. To put a section break into a document use *Insert-Break* and from the following dialog box select a section break from the choices available.

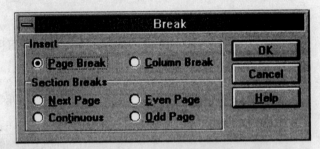

❑ A section break may be chosen so that it starts on the next page, or that there is no apparent break, this is the **Continuous** option.

❑ To start a new section on the next page then select the **Next Page** option.

❑ If the document is to be printed on both sides of the page then it may be desirable to start a new section on either the next odd or even page. This choice can be made by clicking on the appropriate option button.

Word separates each section with a section break, which appears as a double dotted line across the screen with the text 'End of Section' in its centre. A new section should be created when a change occurs in the document, for example,

❑ The number of newspaper-style columns on a page.

❑ The alignment of the text, portrait or landscape.

❑ The format, sequence and position of page numbering.

❑ The text and formatting of headers and footers.

Applying different formatting to individual sections

Once the document has been divided up into sections then different formatting may be applied.

Headers and footers

Using *View-Header and Footer* and the **Page** Setup button you can specify the types of headers and footers required in each section of your document. If the headers or footers is the same as that in the previous section then click on the **Same as Previous** button. Two headers are illustrated below, the header area is enclosed by a dashed bounding rectangle with information as to the type of header, the section number and whether it is the same as the previous header.

```
.Even Page Header ·Section 7·- - - - - - - - - - - - - - - - - - - - - - - - - - - - - - -Same as Previous- -
|Session·5:·Large·documents¶                                                                |
'- - - - - - - - - - - - - - - - - - - - - - - - - - - - - - - - - - - - - - - - - - - - - -'
```

```
.Odd Page Header ·Section 7·- - - - - - - - - - - - - - - - - - - - - - - - - - - - - - - - - - -
|               →                        ·Activity·5.6:·Dividing·the·document·into·sections¶|
'- - - - - - - - - - - - - - - - - - - - - - - - - - - - - - - - - - - - - - - - - - - - - -'
```

Footers are shown in a similar way.

exercise 5.12

This exercise shows how different headers and footers may be applied to different sections of a document. Open the document **Report**

❒ Position the insertion point at the left of the F of the heading Findings from Market research.

❒ Choose *Insert-Break*.

❒ Click on **Next Page** section break. A double dotted line with the text End of Section appears on the screen above the heading.

❒ Use *View-Header and Footer*, click on the **Page Setup** button and check that **Different First Page** does *not* have an X in its box. Click on **OK**.

❒ In the Section 2 header overwrite the heading set up in exercise 5.5 with the text Findings. Click on **Close**.

❒ Save the document as **Report**. Use *File-Print Preview* in **Two Pages** mode to view the document. Print out the last two pages.

Page numbering

Each section may have its own page numbering. To customise a section make sure the insertion point is in the section to be customised. Use *Insert-Page Numbers* and alter the page numbering through the **Page Number Format** dialog box.

Page layout

Different sections may have different formatting, for example the orientation, page size or the number of columns can alter. Note that styles remain the same regardless of section breaks. If you want to use different fonts in a particular section then define additional style names. In Session 8 formatting documents with newspaper style columns will be discussed.

exercise 5.13

Start a new document, this two page document will have the first page in portrait orientation and the second in landscape. Key in the following text:

CHELMER LEISURE AND RECREATION CENTRE

M E M O R A N D U M

To: All Multi-gym Staff   Date: 8 October 199X

From: Geoff Richards

MULTI-GYM ACTIVITY PROGRAMME

Further to last Wednesday's meeting I have completed the activity timetable for the multi-gym. A copy is attached to this memo. Thank you for your hard work and co-operation in devising activity programmes to be used in the multi-gym.

- ❏ Press **ENTER** to make a new line and use *Insert-Break* to insert a **Section Break** starting on the **Next Page**.

- ❏ Select a landscape orientation using *File-Page Setup*, click on the **Paper Size** 'index card label' and in the orientation section click on **Landscape**.

- ❏ Using *Insert-File* insert the document **Timetble** created in exercise 4.14. Adjust the table to fill the page. Note that you will need to scroll left and right to view the width of the page, or use the **Zoom** facility to 'shrink' the view.

- ❏ View the document using *File-Print Preview* in **Two Pages** mode. The first page should be displayed in portrait orientation and the second in landscape. Print out the document.

activity 5.7 Creating a simple table of contents

Most large documents have headings. Some headings are more important than others for example a chapter heading is more important than a paragraph heading. Word allows eight heading styles to be defined. Heading 1 is the most important and Heading 8 is the least important. Usually 2 or 3 heading styles are enough for a document.

By defining and using the heading styles for your documents, not only is consistency maintained but Word is also able to use them to create a table of contents. This is best illustrated in the following exercise.

exercise 5.14

A simple table of contents is to be created for the document **Report**.

❏ Open the document **Report**.

❏ Choose and define a style for Heading 1.

❏ Apply this style to the heading at the top of each page.

❏ Save the document.

❏ Position the insertion point where the table is to go. Tables of contents may be put anywhere, but it is advisable to choose the end of the document. By putting a page break at the end of the document and inserting the table of contents after it, page numbering is unaffected.

❏ Use **CTRL+END** to move to the end of the document. Insert a page break or better still key in CONTENTS and format this with Page Break Before.

❏ Position the cursor under CONTENTS and choose **Insert-Index and Tables** and click on **Table of Contents** 'tab'.

❏ Select a format for the table of contents and click on **OK**. The table of contents will be inserted.

❏ Save the document as **Report**. Should the document be revised the table of contents can be updated by positioning the insertion point in the table of contents and pressing F9. You will be given the choice of updating either just the page numbers or the whole table of contents.

Note: you can use a table of contents to 'jump' to a specific heading in your document, by double clicking on the page number of the heading you wish to go to.

Session 6
Charts in documents

objectives

At the end of this Session you will be able to:

☐ **enter Graph** and **import a chart** into a Word document

☐ **create a chart**

☐ **enter data into a datasheet**

☐ **select the chart type**

☐ **format a chart**

☐ **add and format chart text**

☐ **format other features of charts**

Familiarity with such operations will allow you to develop a confidence with the creation and use of charts in Word documents. There is only space in this chapter for a very quick review of the options for creating charts. However, once you have grasped the basics of chart design it is relatively easy to explore additional features independently.

Graph is a charting application that is embedded in Word. Graph makes it very easy to create business graphics such as graphs, bars, pie charts and similar data display formats, and to insert these directly into a Word document such as a report, presentation or newsletter.

activity 6.1 Creating a chart and importing a chart into a Word document

This activity shows you how to create a simple graph and insert it into a Word document.

Entering Graph

To enter Graph, with a Word document open, click on the Graph icon on the toolbar. The screen will display a linked data sheet and chart which may show the default chart. Data entered on the data sheet will be displayed on the chart.

The Datasheet Window

		A	B	C	D	E
		1st Qtr	2nd Qtr	3rd Qtr	4th Qtr	
1	East	20.4	27.4	90	20.4	
2	West	30.6	38.6	34.6	31.6	
3	North	45.9	46.9	45	43.9	
4						

Document2 - Datasheet

The Datasheet Window is like a simple spreadsheet worksheet. Labels for data are entered in the first row and column of the data sheet. Do not type data in these cells. This first row and column remain visible as you scroll the sheet. Various parts of the datasheet have names that we will use later. The important components of the datasheet are:

The Components of the Datasheet Window

row and column headings	above the first row and to the left of the first column of the data sheet
cell	one rectangle of the data sheet
active cell	currently selected cell
data point	single cell value
data series	a row or column of data used to plot one set of bars, columns, one line, or one pie
series names	names that identify each row and column of data
tick mark labels	when the data series are in rows, the tick mark labels are the column labels. When data series are in columns, the tick mark labels are the row labels
double lines	indicate separate data series

The Chart

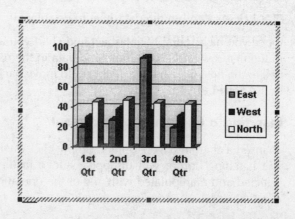

The data in the form of a chart appears in the document. Again, parts of the chart have names that will be used later. The important components of the chart are:

The Components of the Chart

chart	the entire areas inside the chart window
data marker	a bar, shape or dot that marks a single data point or value
data series	a group of related data points
axis	a line that serves as a reference for plotting data on a chart
tick mark	a small line that intersects the axis and marks off a category
plot area	the area in which Graph plots the data
gridlines	lines that extend from the tick marks across the chart
chart text	text that describes data or items in a chart
legend	the key

Managing Datasheet Window and Chart

All of the operations that can normally be performed on windows can be performed on the data sheet window. It can be sized by moving its borders, or moved by dragging the title bar to a new position.

To work with the chart click on it and the icons on the toolbar will change to provide a range of charting tools. Once you have clicked on the chart the datasheet window will disappear. To redisplay the datasheet window click on the **View Datasheet** icon on the toolbar.

Creating a Simple Chart

To create a simple chart you merely need to enter data into the data sheet. If you already have the default data and chart on your screen, you will first need to clear this. This can be achieved by:

❏ Selecting the datasheet, by clicking in the top left hand box. The datasheet should be highlighted in black.

❏ Choose **Edit-Clear**, followed by **All**.

❏ Click on a cell in the datasheet to de-select it.

Once you have a empty datasheet and chart you are ready to begin. Enter labels in the first row and first column and data in the remaining cells. Move from one cell to the next by using the **TAB** key. To move backwards from one cell to another use **SHIFT+TAB**.

Inserting a Chart into a Document

To insert a chart into a document, simply click on the document outside the chart. The hatching border will disappear. Once in the document the chart may be selected and manipulated with any of the operations that can be applied to any other selection or object, such as moving, copying, cutting, pasting, sizing and justification.

Saving a Chart

Charts are saved as part of the document in which they are embedded. To save a chart place the chart in a document and save the document in the normal way using *File-Save*. Note that the chart, the data and all formats are saved as part of your document.

Printing a Chart

Charts are also printed as part of the document in which they are embedded. Print the document in the normal way using *File-Print Preview* to view the document first, and then **PRINT**.

Editing a Chart

To edit a chart:

❑ double click on the chart in your document.

❑ to display the datasheet click on the *View Datasheet* icon in the toolbar. Make whatever changes you wish to the chart or the data.

❑ when finished click on the main document and save, as described previously.

exercise 6.1

We wish to create a simple chart showing one dataseries, as shown below. This chart shows the use of the multi-gym by different categories of users during the week ending 19/04/92. To create this chart:

❑ Click on the Graph icon, to enter Graph. The default Datasheet and Chart should be displayed.

❑ If necessary clear the default graph as indicated above.

❑ Enter the following data in the second row in the chart with the labels in the first row, leaving the first column blank.

Senior	Junior	Concessionary	Senior Club	Junior Club
26	2	23	12	9

❑ Note that at this point we can not see all the labels in the first row.

❑ Click on the Chart Window to examine your chart. It currently lacks a title and axes labels and would benefit from further formatting. We will attend to this later.

❑ Insert your chart in your document by clicking outside it.

❑ Save the document, with its embedded chart using the filename **Users,** by choosing *File-Save*.

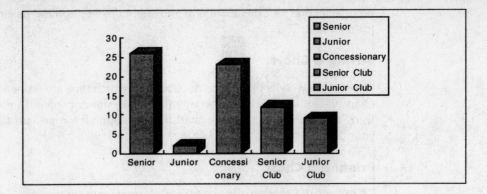

Creating Two or More Copies of a Chart

Once you have inserted a chart into a document you may create an additional copy by cutting and pasting thus:

❏ Select chart

❏ Choose **Edit-Copy**

❏ Move the insertion point to where you wish to insert the second copy of the chart in your document

❏ Choose **Edit-Paste**.

This operation can also be used to transfer charts between documents, if you have two or more documents open in separate windows.

A copy of the chart may be edited as indicated above and used to create another chart based on the same or related data. Thus several different displays can be created showing the same or different subsets of the same data series.

exercise 6.2

The objective of this exercise is to create two copies of a chart, and then to reformat the second chart. To do this:

❏ Select your chart in your document **Users** by clicking on it.

❏ Make a second copy using **Edit-Copy**, move the cursor to the position for the second copy and use **Edit-Paste**.

❏ Double click on the second copy, to enter Graph.

❏ Make the Datasheet Window active by clicking on the **View Datasheet** icon.

❏ Add the following data in the next row of the datasheet.

42	3	31	6	9

❏ Examine the new chart. Two data series should now be displayed as below.

❏ Update the chart in the document. Note that you now have two versions of your chart in your document. Save the document again as **Users**.

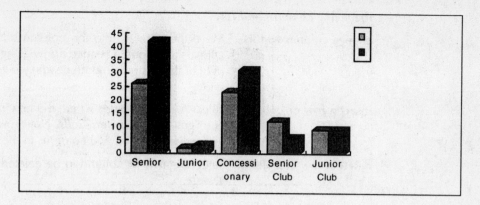

activity 6.2 Working with the data sheet

The data sheet is like a simple worksheet in a spreadsheet package. You will need to be able to move around the data sheet, edit the values in cells, define the data series to be displayed, change column widths, clear, move and copy data and insert and delete rows and columns. The following table summarises some of the key operations.

Datasheet Operations

To	Do this
selection	
select a cell	click on the cell
select a range of cells	point to the first cell, and drag through the remaining cells
select a row or column	click on the heading cell at the side of a row or at the top of a column.
select entire datasheet	click on blank square in upper left corner of the datasheet
entering and editing data	
enter data	select cell, type data and press **ENTER**
edit data	double click on cells so that its contents appear in the **Cell Data** dialog box. Position insertion point, edit, and choose **OK** to enter edits into the cell
clear cell contents	select cells. Choose *Edit-Clear*. decide whether you wish to clear data, format or both data and format. Choose **Clear Data, Clear Format** or **Clear Both** button accordingly
undoing changes	choose *Edit-Undo*

managing columns and rows

change column widths   Move the pointer onto the column boundary until it appears as a double headed arrow. Drag the line to the right of the desired column heading to give the desired width

insert a row or column   select row or columns where the new row or column is to go. Choose **Insert-Cells**. Note rows are inserted above the selection and columns to the left.

delete a row or column   select the row or column to be deleted. Choose **Edit-Delete**.

moving and copying data

move data   select cells. Choose **Edit-Cut**. Select upper left cell of paste area. Choose **Edit-Paste.**

copy data   select cells, Choose **Edit-Copy**. Select upper left cell of paste area. Choose **Edit-Paste.**

exercise 6.3

Using the second chart in the document **Users**, we wish to improve the format of the datasheet so that it appears similar to the datasheet displayed below. Here are some functions to try:

❏ Widen the columns so that the labels in the first row can be displayed clearly, by placing the pointer on the column boundary and dragging the column line to the right of the desired column heading to give an appropriate width.

❏ Enter the following dates in the first column against the respective rows of data: 19/04/92, and 16/08/92.

❏ Enter additional data for the following three weeks in the next three rows, as shown:

06/12/92	40	9	14	13	4
07/02/93	39	12	15	6	7
23/09/93	56	5	16	8	6

❏ Insert a new column between the Junior Club and Senior Club columns to accommodate the following data by clicking on the Junior Club heading cell and using **Insert-Cells**:

Youth Club	0	4	8	10	21

❏ Widen the column as necessary to accommodate the heading.

❏ Move the column with Junior Club heading next to the column with Junior as a heading, by first making a blank column in the appropriate place. Click on the heading cell at the top of the Concessionary column and choose *Insert-Cells.* Select the cells in the Junior Club column by clicking and dragging, then put them on the Clipboard using *Edit-Cut*. Next click on the top cell in the new empty column and choose *Edit -Paste*.

❏ Move the Senior Club column adjacent to the Senior column in a similar way.

❏ Your datasheet should now show the following data:

	Senior	Senior Club	Junior	Junior Club	Concessionary	Youth Club
19/4/92	26	12	2	9	23	0
16/8/92	42	6	3	9	31	4
6/12/92	40	13	9	4	15	8
7/2/93	39	6	12	7	16	10
23/9/93	56	8	5	6	19	21

❏ Examine your chart. It is now attempting to display too much data and does not look very effective. We would like to choose which data to display. For now, simply click in your document, and save the it again as **Users**.

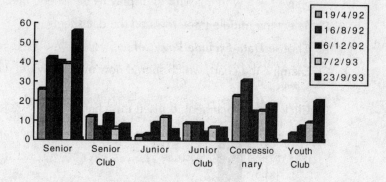

Determining which data is displayed on the chart

In your first chart design you will have accepted the default arrangement which is that all data on the datasheet is displayed on the chart, and that each row is regarded as one data series. Often you may wish to be more selective and display only some of the data in one chart, and other data on a later chart (see creating two copies of charts earlier). Two commands are useful in this context:

Data The Data menu offers the opportunity to define which sets of data should by displayed as a dataseries. Two important options that are self-explanatory are:

Data-Series in Columns

Data-Series in Rows

Excluding and Including Data These options control the data that will appear on the chart, so that data may remain on the datasheet but need not appear on the chart. To exclude data select a row or column. Choose *Data-Exclude Row/Column*. Select **Exclude Rows** or **Exclude Columns** from the dialog box, and choose **OK**. Note that the excluded data row or column is no longer displayed on the chart, and appear dimmed on the datasheet and that the heading cell for excluded columns or rows loses its 'button-like' appearance.

A quicker method of excluding is to double click the row heading cell to the left of the row or column heading cell above the column.

Once excluded, rows or columns can be included again by a similar process.

exercise 6.4

This exercise again uses the chart and datasheet that you have embedded in the document saved as **Users**. Open the document and double-click on the last graph with which you were working. We observed at the end of Exercise 6.3 that the chart was currently showing too many data series to be effective. So we would like to be more selective and to create a series of charts that show selected data series. Suppose, for example, that we wish to compare the attendance data for the first and last weeks shown. Alternatively we might like to compare Junior Club data with Junior data. We will create two charts to display such data.

To create a chart comparing the first and last weeks, double click on the chart that you have been working with to display its datasheet, then:

☐ Select the middle three rows on the datasheet.

☐ Choose **Data-Exclude Row/Col**

☐ Examine the chart, which should now only show the data for the first and last weeks.

☐ Click in the document to insert this chart.

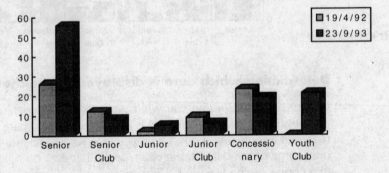

Note that the labels are not fully displayed, this is dealt with in Activity 6.4. Now we wish to create a chart comparing Junior and Junior club data:

☐ To create other charts based on the same datasheet, create an additional copy of the chart as in Exercise 6.2 using **Edit-Copy** and **Edit-Paste**.

☐ Double-click on the new copy of the chart to enter Graph again and click on the **View Datasheet** icon to display the datasheet once more.

☐ Include the excluded rows, using **Data-Include Row/Col**.

☐ Exclude all Columns that you do not wish to display in this chart using **Data-Exclude Row/Col**.

❐ Examine the chart, which should now simply compare the data for Juniors with that for the Junior Club, but you should see that it needs re-arranging.

 ❐ Click on the **By Column** icon in the toolbar for a more acceptable display. Examine the new chart.

❐ Insert this chart in the document. Save the document as **Users**.

Formatting cells

The appearance of cells in the datasheet can be changed by modifying font, size, style and the colour of data in a cell. There are a number of numerical formats that can be adopted, for example, currency signs, different numbers of decimal places and thousands separators. Numerical values next to tick marks can be changed by defining or changing the number format of the cell in the second column of the second row of the datasheet. All of the Format options are shown on the **Format** menu.

exercise 6.5

Using the datasheet associated with the chart that you were working with in Exercise 6.4, experiment with formatting the cells, using the options on the **Format** menu. For example you might try:

❐ Using **Format-Font** to change the font and size of the text.

❐ Using **Format-Number** to choose different date formats for the first column.

Save your changes if you prefer them to the original.

activity 6.3 Changing Chart Type and Format

Graph offers a number of different means for formatting charts. This activity starts to explore some of the options by indicating possible chart types and formatting options. Other features of charts that can be manipulated and changed include chart text, gridlines, arrows, legend(key) axis, data chart markers and data marker patterns. These are reviewed in activity 6.4 and activity 6.5

To date we have used the default chart format which is the column chart. To explore other formats that are available, click on the down arrow of the **Chart Type** icon or use **Format-Chart Type** and select a chart type.

Options include: bar, area, column, line, pie, combination, XY scatter, 3-D area, 3-D bar, 3-D column, 3-D pie and 3-D line. The chart format can also be changed by choosing an appropriate option. For example, the **Options** button in the **Chart Type** dialog box shows a range of chart formats.

Note: It is important to choose chart type first as any subsequent formatting applies to a specific chart type. Should you have already added formatting to your chart and find that you wish to change its type, then you should do so by using **Format-Chart Type**.

exercise 6.6

Using the last chart that you created experiment with displaying the data in different formats and chart types, by investigating the options under *Chart Type*. Note that some chart types are more suitable than others for your data. Good charts are charts that suit their purpose. To add data labels as illustrated use *Insert-Data labels* and choose **Show Value**.

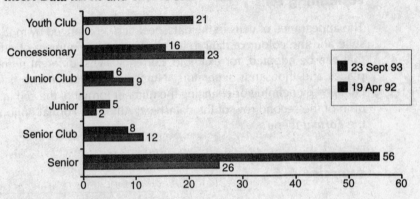

Hints for good charts

Since there is a wide range of different chart types available the most difficult decision is the choice of the correct chart type to effectively display a specific data series. To some extent this is a matter of personal preference, but the set of hints below offers some general guidelines that you may wish to consider. Some of these hints relate to points that you will master in Activities 6.4 and 6.5, but they are summarised here for completeness.

1. Think about the appearance of the chart when it is printed on paper. It is easy to get carried away when you are designing a chart on a coloured screen. Think about whether the data series that are shown will be sufficiently differentiated when printed on a non-colour printer. Test this.

2. Do not display too many data series on one chart; three is often sufficient.

3. When using bar or column charts distinguish between when composite and normal bar or column charts are appropriate. Think about which data you are comparing with which other data.

4. Use 3-D charts sparingly. Only simple 3-D charts look effective on paper.

5. Only use pie charts to display parts of a whole. It is inadvisable to explode more than one segment. The format which is often most helpful shows data labels and %'s.

6. Use line graphs to join distinct data points. Use different data markers to denote different data series.

7. Check that the chart has a title, axes labels, data!, and, when more than one data series is displayed, a legend.

8. Try not to cover data markers with text such as titles or the legend. If necessary move text and legend.

9. Examine the chart for legibility. Turn the tick mark labels round or change their size if necessary,

10. Remember that the most effective charts often show a very limited set of data, effectively labelled.

11. Only use gridlines sparingly.

12. When creating a number of charts in a document, try to develop a style so that comparable data appears on a similarly formatted chart.

activity 6.4 Working with chart text

Charts need to be clearly labelled. Some text is placed on the chart by Graph. We may wish to delete, or edit, this text, and add other text. Typically text on a chart includes chart titles, axes labels, data marker labels and other text. Text can be attached or unattached. Typical attached text includes chart titles, axes labels and data marker labels. Unattached text may be moved freely to any position on the chart. The following table summarises the key operations that you may wish to perform on chart text.

Operations on Chart Text

To	Do this
Add attached text	Choose **Insert-Titles**. Select the appropriate part of the chart to which you wish to add text. Choose **OK**. Type in text. The text appears in white selection squares. Press **ESC**
Add unattached text	Type the text required. The text appears in black squares indicating that you can move and size the text. Press **ESC**
Select text	Click on the text
Edit text	Select text, then retype it, or position the insertion point within the text and insert or delete characters. Press **ESC**
Delete text	Select text, and choose **Edit-Clear**
Move unattached text	Select text, and click between the selection squares to show the border surrounding the text, drag to the position that you want
Display data labels, values or percentages	Switch to Chart window. Choose **Insert-Data Labels**, and select appropriate options. Choose **OK**

The chart text font, alignment and orientation can be changed. in addition it is possible to change the pattern and colour of the text area and the colour, weight and style of the border around the text. To illustrate this process we will consider changing the orientation of axis labels on the x-axis from horizontal to vertical. To do this:

❏ select the axis

❏ choose **Format-Selected Axis**

❏ under Orientation in **Alignment**, select the text orientation you want

❏ to format the font of the text, choose the **Font** tab and select the options that you want

❏ choose **OK**.

exercise 6.7

It is time that we added some axis labels and a title to our chart and investigated any other formatting that might be necessary. In the document **Users** double-click on the chart that compares Junior data with Junior Club Data. We will add some labels to this, so that it starts to look like the chart below.

❏ Once you are in Graph click on the chart to select it.

❏ Choose **Insert-Titles** and select **Chart**, and **OK**. Type in the text e.g. Attendance Figures. This appears in white selection squares. To remove these squares, press **ESC.**

❏ Choose **Insert-Titles**, then **Category [X] Axis** from the dialog box. Type in the text e.g. Week Commencing. This appears in white selection squares. To remove these squares, press **ESC.**

❏ Choose **Insert-Titles**, then **Value [Z] Axis**. Type in the text e.g. Number, and press **ESC** to remove the selection squares. Change the orientation of this text.

❏ You will observe that adding labels tends to shrink the size of the chart display. Stretch the chart to a suitable size taking care not to exceed the margins.

❏ The chart as shown below also features some additional formatting as described in Exercise 6.8.

❏ Insert the chart into the document **Users,** and save the document.

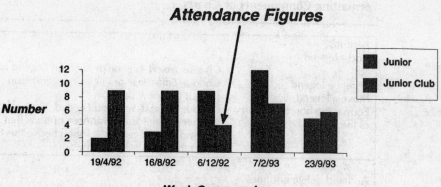

Attendance Figures

activity 6.5 More Chart Formatting

Every feature of a chart can be modified or formatted in the same way. Many of the options to perform these operations are under the Insert and Format menus. First, however, before you can format or edit a chart item it must be selected.

When a chart item is selected it is marked with either black squares or black squares and a border, depending upon its type. Chart items and text marked with black squares or handles and a border can be formatted with commands and moved or sized with the mouse. Chart items and text marked with only selection squares cannot be moved or sized directly. Some items, such as axis labels, can be formatted or realigned with commands. It is useful to review the means for selecting parts of charts.

Selecting chart items

To	Do this
Select an item	Click on the item
Select a series	Click any marker in the series
Select a single data marker	To format a single data marker, click it once to select the series, again to select the individual marker, and then double-click it to display the Format Data Point dialog box.
Select gridlines	Click on a gridline
Select axis	Click the area containing the axis tick mark labels
Select the entire plot area	Click any area in the plot area not occupied by another item
Select the entire chart	Click anywhere outside the plot area, where there is not another item.

The table below summarises some of the key operations necessary in order to format legends, gridlines, arrows, axes and data markers:

Formatting Components of Charts

Legends	
Add a legend	Choose **Insert-Legend** or click on Legend icon
Delete a legend	Choose **Edit-Clear** or click on legend icon.
Move a legend	Drag it to a new position
Format the border and area of the legend box	Choose **Format-Selected Legend**. Under the **Patterns** tab select the Border and Area options that you want. To format the legend text font, choose the **Font** tab, and select the options that you want
Gridlines	
Add and delete gridlines	Click on either or both the gridlines icons.
Format gridlines	Select one of the major gridlines for the axis, and choose **Format-Selected gridline**. Select the style, colour and weight, and choose **OK**
Arrows	
Add an arrow	Display the Drawing toolbar by clicking on the Drawing icon and click on the Arrow icon.
Clear an arrow	Choose **Edit-Clear**
Move an arrow	Drag it
Size and change the direction of an arrow	Select and drag the handles
Axes	
Format the axes scale	Click on axis to be formatted. Choose **Format-Selected axis** and choose the **Scale** tab. Enter the appropriate values or select or clear boxes to achieve the scale format required
Format axes patterns and tick mark label location	Select an axis to be formatted. Choose **Format-Selected axis** and choose the **Patterns** tab. This will cause the **Axis Pattern** dialog box to be displayed. Under *Axis* select type, style, colour and weight for the axis line. Under *Tick Mark Type*, select the alignment for tick marks. Under *Tick Labels*, select the position on the chart where the tick labels are to appear. To format the tick mark label font choose the **Font** tab. To format the orientation of the tick mark labels, choose **Alignment** tab and select the options that you want. To format the axis scale choose the **Scale** tab. Choose **OK**.
Data Markers	
Format data marker layout	Choose **Insert-Data labels**. Select the options that you wish to apply to your chart, and choose **OK**.
Format the border and area of the data markers	Select the marker to format. Choose **Format-Selected data label**. Select the font, alignment, border and area options required. Choose **OK**
Clear the data marker format	Select the marker, and choose **Edit-Clear**. Select the **All** option, and choose **OK**

exercise 6.8

The objective of this exercise is to encourage you to explore some of the formatting features of Graph. There is not space here to deal with these in detail, but here are a few things that have been used on the chart above and which you might like to try:

- ❑ Select the chart that you were working with in Exercise 6.7.

- ❑ Select the title by clicking on it (the border with black selection squares are displayed). Choose **Format-Selected chart title** and choose **Font** then change the format of the text to, say, Italic and a larger font size.

- ❑ Select each of the axes label in turn. Choose **Format-Selected...** and change the format of the text using the **Font** tab.

- ❑ Select each of the axes in turn. Choose **Format-Selected axis** and choose **Patterns**. In the dialog box, change the **Tick Mark Type** for **Major** to **Cross** and for **Minor** to **None**. Set the **Tick Mark Labels** at **Low**.

- ❑ Move the legend by first clicking on it to select it and then dragging it to a better position.

- ❑ Add an arrow, by clicking on the **Arrow** icon in the drawing toolbar and drawing the arrow by dragging. Position the arrow by moving the two ends in turn.

- ❑ Examine and insert your chart in the document and save the document again as **Users**.

activity 6.6 Editing a chart

The *Edit* menu can be used for manipulating charts as for pieces of text. First click on the chart to select it, then you can copy or clear a chart or undo changes to a chart as described below.

Copying a chart

To copy a chart choose **Edit-Copy Chart**. Graph copies the chart to the clipboard. Switch to the application where you want to position the chart. Choose **Edit-Paste**.

Clearing a chart

To clear a chart select the entire chart in the Chart window. Choose **Edit-Clear**. Choose the **All**, **Formats** or **Data** option button depending upon whether you wish to clear both data and formats or only formats or only data.

Undoing changes

To reverse changes use **Edit-Undo**.

Note: There are no direct exercises attached to this activity, but you should find these operations useful in managing the charts in the other exercises.

integrative exercises

exercise 6.9

Traffic Consultants, Fogg and Co are concerned for the local residents in the vicinity of Kibbleworth and commission a study of the number of commercial and private vehicles travelling along the main access road. Create a chart displaying the following data and insert the chart in a document:

	Sun	Mon	Tues	Wed	Thurs	Fri	Sat
Private	33	34	51	47	63	19	39
Commercial	1	26	25	20	37	15	12

First create a column chart showing both data series. Do not forget to add axes labels and a title. Format the title and the axes labels appropriately. Format any other features of the chart that you would like to change, such as the axes. Insert the chart into your document. Make a further copy of the chart and use the datasheet associated with this copy to create two more charts.

Select each data series in turn ie Private, and then Commercial and display each of these on separate bar charts, both of which you should insert into your document. Choose appropriate formatting and check that the axes labels and title are appropriate.

exercise 6.10

Use a Pie chart to display the following data concerning the use of a health and fitness centre in 1995:

Step Aerobics	Popmobility	Aerobics	Keep Fit
5058	4779	2080	679

Remember to add a title and experiment with the use of data labels, possibly as percentages. Save this chart in a document called **Aerobics.**

objectives

Word allows a graphic image to be created and inserted into a document. Graphic images are integral parts of many documents and the drawing toolbar offers a means to construct them from within the word processor.

In this session the basic features of the drawing toolbar will be explored. At the end of the session you should be able to create:

☐ basic shapes from which images can be created

☐ simple images and diagrams

☐ images incorporating text

☐ images using colour and patterns

☐ a logo

Drawings are invaluable in many documents for example in presenting plans or layouts. Box and line diagrams are widely used in many scientific and technical documents.

Cartoons can be used to introduce an element of fun into a drawing. The drawing functions of word make it easier to incorporate company logos into letters or documents.

If so desired, images can be imported and this will be considered in the last part of this session.

activity 7.1 Displaying the drawing toolbar

The drawing toolbar can only be used from an open document, therefore either start a new document or open an existing one.

Position the insertion point at the point in your document where the drawing is to be. Click on the **DRAWING ICON** in the tool bar. The document will switch to a Page Layout view and the drawing toolbar is displayed at the bottom of the screen. Clicking on the drawing button in the main toolbar will toggle the display of the drawing toolbar. The buttons on the toolbar are the drawing tools and functions.

Drawings can be created either directly in page layout or they can be created as a picture. In page layout view you may draw directly on the text on your document. The drawing can remain fixed at that position on the page or it can be anchored to a paragraph so that it will move with the text. This sort of drawing is only visible in page layout view.

 A drawing may be created as a picture and for diagrams in a document this is the best method as the picture is a separate entity, also this kind of picture is visible in normal view. To create a picture click on the **Create Picture** button in the drawing toolbar and a drawing workspace will be displayed.

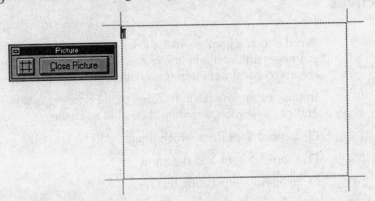

You can create your picture within the boundary shown, or if your drawing element is outside the boundary click on the **Reset Picture Boundary** button to enclose all drawing elements in the picture boundary. When the picture is complete click on the **Close Picture** button to return to your document.

activity 7.2 Creating basic shapes

Drawing Lines

 Click on the line drawing icon, position the pointer at the start of the line, click and drag to the end of the line. Lines may be freely positioned or they may start and end on invisible grid points. The following exercise investigates how the **Snap to Grid** button on the drawing toolbar can be used to control this.

exercise 7.1

Start a new document and click on the **DRAWING ICON**. Click on the **Create Picture** button on the toolbar to display the drawing workspace. Note that all the exercises will create drawing as separate entities but if so wished you may draw directly on your document in Page Layout view.

❏ Click on the line drawing tool. In the drawing area the pointer changes to a +.

❏ Position the pointer near the top of the area enclosed by the drawing boundary, click and drag towards the bottom of the drawing area. Don't release the mouse button just yet; notice how the line follows your pointer movements in a rather jerky fashion.

❑ Release the mouse button and a line is drawn.

 Click on the **Snap to Grid** button on the drawing toolbar. This displays the **Snap to Grid** dialog box.

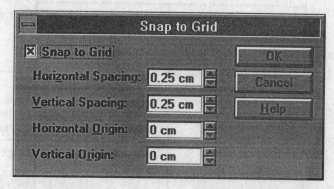

Notice that the **Snap to Grid** check box is checked. This is the reason for the jerkiness of the line positioning. When **Snap to Grid** is **checked** lines start and finish on invisible grid points.. This is useful for maintaining consistency in a drawing. Through the **Snap to Grid** dialog box the spacing of the invisible grid can be customised.

Remove the x in the **Snap to Grid** check box and repeat the line drawing exercise. This time notice that the end of the line should follow your pointer movements smoothly.

 Different line styles may be selected by clicking on the **Line Style** button in the toolbar. A menu of styles appears which can be selected from or the **Drawing Defaults** dialog box can be displayed by clicking on **More**.

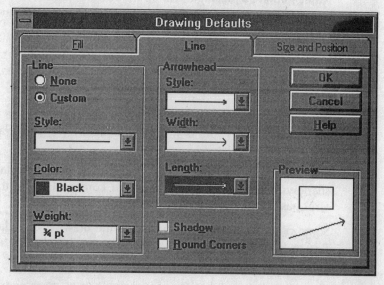

Click on the **Close Picture** button to return to the document. Save the document as **Doodle**. Once a drawing is embedded in a document it can be manipulated in the same way as an embedded chart, i.e. its size can be changed and it may be cut, copied and pasted.

Drawing ellipses, circles, rectangles, and squares

The methods for drawing these shapes are summarised in the following table.

Ellipse/Circle	Rectangle/square	
To draw an ellipse from the corner of an imaginary bounding box	To draw a rectangle from one corner	Click on appropriate tool icon, position pointer at corner and drag to size required
To draw an ellipse from its centre	To draw a rectangle from its centre	Click on appropriate tool icon, hold down the **CTRL** key, position pointer at centre and drag to size required
To draw a circle from the corner of an imaginary bounding box	To draw a square from one corner	Click on appropriate tool icon, hold down the **SHIFT** key, position pointer at centre and drag to size required
To draw a circle from its centre	To draw a square from its centre	Click on appropriate tool icon, hold down the **CTRL** and **SHIFT** keys, position pointer at centre and drag to size required

Note: To draw a rectangle with rounded corners check the Round Corners check box in the **Drawing Defaults** dialog box. A shadowed object can be constructed if the **Shadow** check box is checked.

exercise 7.2

Open the document **Doodle**, position the pointer in the drawing and double-click. This displays your drawing in the picture workspace and allows the chosen drawing to be updated.

Create each of the shapes described in the preceding table. Experiment with shadows and rectangles with rounded corners. Explore the effect that **Snap to Grid** has on the way in which the shapes are created.

Some of your shapes may go outside the drawing boundary, if so, click on the **Resize Boundary** button. Save this drawing by clicking on **Close Picture** and using *File-Save* for revision in later exercises.

Drawing arcs

By clicking on the arc drawing button the pointer can be used to draw 90° segments (quadrants) of ellipses or circles. The arc may be filled, in which case it looks like a wedge, or unfilled in which case it is only the edge of the ellipse. To select whether the arc is filled or unfilled display the **Drawing Defaults** dialog box and choose the 'Fill' tab and choose from the options shown. A preview of your choice is shown in the bottom right hand corner.

exercise 7.3

In this exercise recall the drawing from the document **Doodle** and add an arc to it.

❐ Position the pointer at one end of where the arc is to begin.

❐ Drag to complete the arc, the direction in which the dragging is done determines which quadrant of an ellipse is drawn. If an arc of a circle is required hold down the **SHIFT** key during the dragging operation.

❐ Use the **Drawing Defaults** dialog box to experiment with line style, fill and colour.

❐ Close the picture and save the document **Doodle**.

Drawing Freeform Shapes

Shapes composed of straight lines and/or freehand lines can be drawn using the Freeform icon. The shapes may be closed, i.e. the beginning and the end is the shape join up or they may be open. A closed shape can be filled with an alternative colour and/or pattern.

Drawing a shape composed of straight lines

Click on the Freeform tool, position the pointer at the start of the shape, click, move the pointer to the end of the first line, click and repeat for each line in the shape. If the shape is closed, a polygon, when drawing the last line, to finish click near the beginning of the first line.

To create an open shape, when it is finished either press **ENTER**, **ESC**, or double click.

Drawing a freehand shape

Click on the Freeform tool, position the pointer at the start of the shape, click and drag to draw the shape. Do not worry if your drawing is shaky or inaccurate, Word offers the facility to edit the drawing, as described in the next activity.

An open or closed shape may be created as for a shape composed of straight lines.

Drawing a shape with both freehand and straight line sections

It is possible to alternate between drawing a straight line or drawing freehand to produce a composite shape. Use the move and click technique for drawing straight lines and a click and drag technique for the freehand sections. Open or closed shapes may be created.

exercise 7.4

In a new drawing to be created underneath the previous one in the document **Doodle** the techniques just described will be experimented with. The aim is to reproduce the image shown below. This image is composed of two closed shapes, the star and the 'leaves' of the tree, and one open shape, the tree trunk.

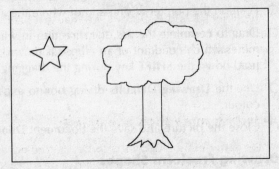

- ❐ Position the insertion point below the previous picture in **Doodle** and click on the **Create Picture** button to start a new picture.
- ❐ Click on the Freeform button, position the pointer to start drawing the star. Hint: check that the **Snap to Grid** option is not checked
- ❐ Click, move to the end of the line, click and repeat until back at the original start position. The closed shape of the star should have been formed.
- ❐ Using the Freeform button again, draw the 'leaves' shape. Position the pointer at the start of the shape.
- ❐ Click and drag to draw the shape. Finish the shape at the original start position so that a closed shape is formed.
- ❐ To create the tree trunk start at the leaves, work down to the base and then back up. Experiment with combining freehand and straight lines to create this shape.
- ❐ As this is an open shape, end the shape by double-clicking.
- ❐ Close the picture and save the document **Doodle**. Preview and print it.

activity 7.3 Editing an Image

It is very unlikely that a drawing will be right first time and parts of it will need to be altered or removed. An image is usually made of several parts, a different drawing tool may have been used to create each part, or there may be several parts created by the same tool. Each part of the drawing is known as an **object.** Each object may be selected and altered individually or objects may be selected together.

Selecting objects – arrow tool

The object which needs to be altered or deleted needs to be selected before changes can be made. The arrow or **Select Drawing Objects** button is used to select the required object. After clicking on this button the pointer changes to an arrow.

Use the arrow to point to the object which is to be altered. If the object is filled then the arrow may be placed anywhere within the bounds of the object, if it is not filled then place the arrow on its frame (outside edge).

If the object is a line, clicking will cause a handle (small black box) to appear at each end. For other objects eight handles will appear. These handles are at the corners and the middle of the sides of an invisible rectangle surrounding the object.

The handles are known as re-sizing handles and can be used to edit the object.

Selecting more than one object

If the same editing action is to be performed on more than one object of the image, then more than one object can be selected. First consider where an imaginary box that would enclose all the objects required, would be. Using the arrow point to one corner of this imaginary box and click and drag, a dotted line box appears, make sure you have surrounded all the objects you wish to select, with this box, before releasing the mouse button.

An alternative method is to select each object in turn whilst holding down the **SHIFT** key.

Removing parts of an image

Select the part (or parts) of the image to be removed or cleared. By using *Edit-Clear* or using the **DELETE** key the selected object(s) will be removed. Don't forget that you can use *Edit-Undo* if this goes wrong!

Moving and copying

Any object or group of objects can be moved from one location to another in a drawing. To move a single object, first select it and by holding down the mouse button the object can be moved to its new position. A *ghost* (a dotted outline of the object) will move across the screen as you move the mouse. Release the mouse button to drop the object in its new place.

To move a group of objects, first select the objects required. Click on any one of the objects in the group and then drag as for a single object.

Any object or group of objects can be copied using the normal *Copy* and *Paste* operation. First select the object or objects to be copied, use *Edit-Copy* and follow with *Edit-Paste*. A copy will be pasted into the drawing and can be moved to the appropriate place.

exercise 7.5

Double click on the drawing created in Exercise 7.4.

❏ Select the star by clicking anywhere on its edge.

❏ Using *Edit-Copy* and *Edit-Paste* make a copy of the star.

❏ Move the copy by dragging it to another position in the image as illustrated below.

❏ Close the picture and save the document.

Resizing an object

To resize an object the resizing handles which appear when it is selected are used. Any one of the handles may be dragged to resize the object, bearing in mind that the object will behave as if it is pinned to the drawing with the opposite corner from the one that is being dragged.

The point at which the object is pinned is known as the anchor point. As an alternative to one of the corners of the bounding box being the anchor point, a central anchor point can be chosen. To do this hold down the **CTRL** key during the resizing operation.

During resizing the object is displayed in the same way as during moving, that is, either as a *ghost*.

Controlling height, width or proportions during resizing

To resize an object so that its proportion of height to width remains the same, hold down the **SHIFT** key while dragging a resize handle diagonally.

To resize an object so that its height or width remains unchanged, drag one of the central side handles.

Grouping objects for editing

If you wish to perform a sizing operation on more than one object then select all the objects required before performing the editing action. Objects may be grouped which reduces the clutter of many sizing handles and also can speed operation as Word works faster with objects that are grouped. To group a set of selected objects click on the **Group** button in the drawing toolbar. When you have finished the editing then the objects may be ungrouped using the **Ungroup** button in the toolbar.

exercise 7.6

Recall the image from the previous exercise. Select one of the stars. By dragging one of the sizing handles make it smaller as illustrated below.

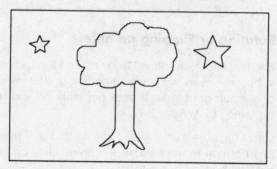

Editing freeform images

All freeform images are composed of lines connected end to end. Even freehand curves are made up of lots of little lines connected end to end. The point at which one line joins to the next is known as a **vertex**.

Before any changes can be made to a freeform it is necessary to display it in editing mode. Select the freeform and click on the **Reshape** button in the toolbar. The freeform is shown with the vertices marked with little control handles.

By dragging the control handles it is possible to edit the freeform. It may be necessary to check that the **Snap to Grid** option is not checked, also it may be useful to zoom in on the drawing (see Activity 7.5). If there are a lot of vertices, they can be deleted. To delete a vertex, position the pointer on the control handle belonging to that vertex, hold down **the CTRL** key and click. A line will join the remaining vertices either side of the one deleted. To add a vertex hold down **SHIFT** and **CTRL** simultaneously and click at the point where one is to be added.

exercise 7.7

Recall the image from the previous exercise.

☐ Select the 'leaves' part of the tree.

❏ Zoom in to part of it and double click on the edge of this freeform to display the control handles.

❏ Drag the control handles to produce more detail in the shape of the freeform object.

❏ Close the drawing and save the document.

Rotating or Flipping an object

Rotating causes an object to be rotated through 90° and flipping causes an object to become its mirror image. Rotating or flipping can be performed on one object or a group of objects. It does not work on text objects, or bitmaps. Bitmaps are explained in Activity 7.7.

Select the object or objects to be rotated or flipped. If rotating click on the **Rotate Right** button in the toolbar, if flipping click on either the **Flip Horizontal** or **Flip Vertical** buttons in the toolbar.

exercise 7.8

Recall the previous image and rotate the left star and flip the right star. Return to the document and save.

activity 7.4 Edges and fills; colour & patterns

Objects such as rectangles, ellipses or other shapes can be drawn with or without edges and fills (it is advisable not to draw lines without edges as they disappear!). Whether an object has an edge or fill when first drawn depends upon the settings in the **Drawing Defaults** dialog box. If changes are made to the defaults then these affect only objects drawn after changes are made.

An object can have different settings from the drawing defaults by double clicking on the object and altering the settings in the **Drawing Object** dialog box (which has the same options as the default dialog box).

Using edging and filling

The style and width of an object's outside edge reflect the default settings of the *Line* section of the **Drawing Defaults** dialog box. The *None* or *Custom* options are used to select whether or not an object has an edge.

A closed object may be filled. Select the object and click on the **Fill Colour** button in the toolbar. Select a colour from the colour grid. Note that this will affect the drawing defaults.

Instead of solid colour fills, shading and patterns may be used. Double click on the object and choose from the patterns options in the *Fill* part of the dialog box.

exercise 7.9

Continuing with the previous drawing, double-click on the 'leaves' object and open the **Patterns** drop down list and select say, Lt Trellis, to fill with a pattern The pattern can be made different colours by selecting from the **Palette Colour** drop down list. To block fill with colour select the object, click on the **Fill Colour** button, and select a colour from the fill palette. Experiment with this.

Overlapping objects

If an image is created where one object overlaps another then the most recently drawn object will obscure the earlier object. Word treats the objects as if they are stacked one on top of another, with most recent on top. This stacking order can be changed by selecting an object and clicking on the **Bring to Front** button in the toolbar to put the object on top of the stack or the **Send to Back** button to send the object to the bottom of the stack.

exercise 7.10

Add a moon created from two circles both without edges, fill one with white and the other with yellow.

Click on the 'leaves' object and click on the **Bring to Front** button to create the following effect.

activity 7.5 Moving around a drawing: zoom

Alternatively choose the level of magnification from the **Zoom Control** drop down list box in the main toolbar. There are seven levels of magnification 10%, 25%, 50%, 75%, 100%, 150%, 200%, Page Width, Whole Page, and Two Pages. If 25% is chosen the image shown is reduced to a quarter of full size, if 200% is chosen the image is shown twice full size. Use the scroll bars to display the required portion of the picture on the screen.

activity 7.6 Images and text

The full range of text fonts available to you within Word are also available to a drawing. Headings and labels can easily be part of the drawing. To put text into an image click on the **Text Box** button in the drawing toolbar and use the point-er to draw a rectangle on the picture into which you can insert text.

Inside the text box will be an insertion point which is where your text will appear as it is keyed in. When the text is complete simply move on to the next action you wish to perform. Whilst the text box is still selected you can perform text formatting using the main tool and formatting bar as usual. For example, the font, size, colour and alignment of the text can be adjusted. The text box itself can have it's edge defined in the same manner as other objects.

Editing Text

To add or correct text within the text box click on the text to place an insertion point in the text, so that additions and corrections can be made.

exercise 7.11

Add text to the drawing as shown:

Activity 7.7 Importing Pictures

Files containing pictures can be created by other applications. A picture file can either be imported directly into a document using *Insert-Picture* or can be imported into a picture workspace in the same way. Two common types of picture file that are created by other Windows applications are formatted as either a bitmap or a Windows metafile. Draw will import other formats as well as these.

A bitmap stores the image as being made up of many tiny squares known as pixels. Other formats store the image as being made up of objects such as lines, ellipses and rectangles, Word is able to 'decode' this information so enabling more flexibility for editing the imported image.

To import a picture use *Insert-Picture* and the following dialog box appears

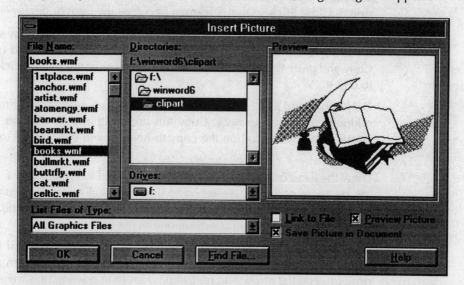

In the **Directories** box, select the directory in which the picture file is situated. From the **File Name** box select the file required. If **Preview Picture** is checked a preview of the selected file is displayed, as illustrated. Note that bitmap files have the extension .bmp and Windows metafile files have the extension .wmf. Other picture files that Word recognises will also be listed in the **File Name** box. After selecting the file click on **OK** and the file will be imported into the document or drawing workspace.

To save the picture in the document, if in the drawing workspace click on **Close Picture**, and save the document.

integrative exercises

exercise 7.12

Start a new document and key in the text for the picture and then display the drawing toolbar and click in the **Create Picture** button. The head is an ellipse and the body is constructed from a series of straight lines. Close the picture and save the document as **Stickman.**

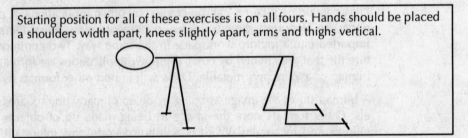

Starting position for all of these exercises is on all fours. Hands should be placed a shoulders width apart, knees slightly apart, arms and thighs vertical.

Start a new document while **Stickman** is open. Select and copy the picture above and paste it into the new document. Save this document as **Stick** for use in session 8. Close **Stick** so that **Stickman** becomes the current document.

In the next part of the exercise two images can be created side by side by putting them into a table. Set up a table that is two columns wide and one row deep. Copy and paste the image above into the first column. Double click on the image to edit it.

Delete the head and back. Redraw half of the back using the arc tool, start at the midpoint and draw to neck. Copy this arc and paste it, click on the **Flip Horizontal** button and position the copy to line up with the original to complete the spine.

Draw the head using the freeform tool as a closed freehand object. Edit this drawing by zooming in and an repositioning the handles on the vertices. Choose a white fill for the head and bring the nearer arm to the front. Add the arrow, by drawing a small line and choosing one of the arrow styles.

Copy the image into the second column. Using the **Flip Vertical** button flip the head and the two parts of the back separately. Select each in turn and move into position. Flip the arrow and reposition. Return to document, save and add another row to the table in which to put the text associated with each diagram. Save the document.

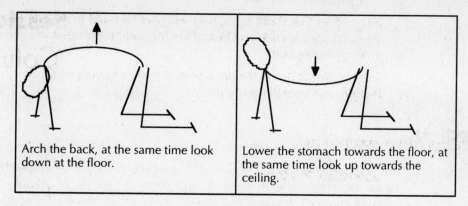

Arch the back, at the same time look down at the floor.

Lower the stomach towards the floor, at the same time look up towards the ceiling.

exercise 7.13 *A logo*

To produce the logo illustrated:

Start a new document and switch to page layout view. Click on the drawing button in the main toolbar.

Click on the text box tool and draw a text box. Choose a thick line for the edge of the box. Add the text.

Click on the ellipse tool and add a circle. Save the document.

Recreate the same logo using the drawing workspace (**Create Picture**). Investigate the differences between the way Word handles the two logos.

Session 8
Columns

objectives

This session helps you to integrate skills that you will have developed by following the exercises earlier in the book, and introduces the use of columns and associated document formatting that might help you to produce a document such as a newsletter. At the end of this session you will be able to:

❐ create a document that uses columns

❐ use section breaks to format different parts of pages separately

❐ create a document that displays any of text, numbers, graphics and pictures on the same page.

Session 5 offered an opportunity to create a long and integrated document, making use of many of the facilities introduced in Sessions 1 to 4. This session is also integrative, but focuses on the creation of relatively short documents, such as newsletters that integrate text, formatted in various ways, with graphics and images. In the design of such documents there is a significant emphasis on the page layout, so it is useful to work in Page View, and to remember to make full use of Print Preview before printing the document. This session creates a short two page newsletter, using some new text and graphics and some text that you will have created in earlier exercises. The principles applied in this session can be extended to longer documents as required.

The newsletter that we wish to create is printed at the end of the text for this session. Note that it is designed to occupy two pages in this book, and is not exactly two pages of A4 in length, since the page size is shorter than A4. Note that the newsletter includes text, text in tables, graphics and an image. There is scope for additional formatting. Here we introduce the basics – you may develop these by, for instance, applying more ambitious border design or shading. The newsletter that you will create in this session is not a real newsletter. It has been designed to allow you to experiment with the use of a range of formatting facilities within columns.

Word is only suitable for the design of simply formatted newsletters. For more ambitious formatting you should examine a desk top publishing package.

Most of the skills that you will need in order to create this newsletter have already been introduced in earlier exercises. We will walk through these operations here for consolidation, and to develop confidence with their use in conjunction with one another. You should be reasonably confident with these earlier exercises, because it is not possible to cover everything that you might do wrong in this session! First, however, you will explore the new concept of columns.

You may find that in this session more than in any of the earlier sessions you have applied some formatting and are unable to retrieve the situation. Do not forget to make use of *Edit-Undo*.

activity 8.1 Working with columns

Word allows you to produce two types of columns. You have already met the columns in tables, which are parallel columns. The second kind of column is the snaking column, in which text flows from the bottom of one column to the top of the next, as in newspaper columns.

Document views

When entering text you will probably have used Normal View most of the time. This is easy for fast text entry, but does not display columns side by side.

Page Layout is preferable when using columns, as it shows columns side by side with items such as graphics, in the correct location. It is useful for editing, manually inserting column breaks, and adjusting column width. You can zoom in or out.

Print Preview shows the overall page layout, just as the document will be printed. You can edit text, and make adjustments to margins and page breaks.

Creating multiple column layout

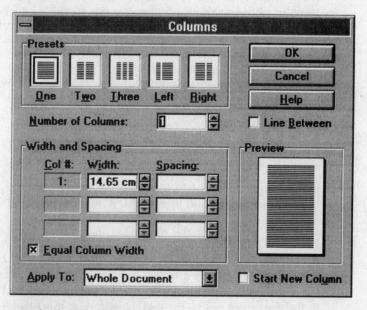

To create a multiple column layout:

❑ Choose *View-Page Layout*

❑ Click in the section to be formatted.

❑ Use *Format-Columns*.

129

- ❏ Specify the number of columns, for example, 2.

- ❏ In the **Apply To** box, select the portion of the document that you want to format

- ❏ Choose **OK**.

Alternatively:

- ❏ Choose *View-Page Layout*

- ❏ Click in the section to be formatted

- ❏ Click on the **Columns** button on the toolbar

- ❏ Drag to the right to select the number of columns that you want.

When you release the mouse button, Word formats the section that contains the insertion point.

You can also use the *Columns* command to:

- ❏ Change the space between columns, through the **Width and Spacing** section

- ❏ Add a vertical line between columns, through the **Line Between** box

- ❏ Format the current section to start in a new column through the **Start New Column** box

You can change the number of columns in all or part of a document. To change the number of columns on part of a document, make that part a separate section by inserting a section break. Within each section Word automatically adjusts the width of the columns. Word adjusts the space between columns to create equal amounts of space. You can customise this for unequal spacing through the **Width and Spacing** section.

Note: Word stores the formatting instructions for a section in the section mark. If you delete a section mark, any text in the section assumes the format of the text below it. If you delete a section break accidentally, do not forget your old friend *Edit-Undo*.

exercise 8.1

In this exercise we wish to set up the basic format for the newsletter. First we wish to add the heading, and then to insert the columns, and finally, we will enter the address at the bottom of page 2.

First open a new document. Check that the correct printer is selected using *File-Print Setup*. Also choose the correct page size using *File-Page Setup*. Choose *View-Page Layout*. Then type 'Chelmer Leisure and Recreation Centre', **ENTER**, 'Fitness News' across the top of the document. Press **ENTER** to make some space in the document below the text. Next format this heading thus:

- ❏ Apply centre justification

- ❏ Select a type font and face that causes the first line to fill the width of the page

- ❏ Format the text to bold

❑ Create some space above and beneath the text (Hint: use a blank line with a smaller point size).

❑ Place a border around the heading by selecting it then using *Format-Borders and Shading*.

Next we wish to create two columns thus:

❑ Place the insertion point below the heading

❑ Choose *Format-Columns*

❑ Select the number of columns below the heading i.e. **2**

❑ Select **Selected text** in the **Apply To** box

❑ Check the **Line Between** check box

❑ Choose **OK**

❑ Word places a section break between the heading and the multiple columns

❑ Finally save this document, using *File-Save*, as **News1**.

exercise 8.2

With the document **News1** open, start to enter the following text at the top of the first column. Format the heading appropriately. Notice that the text is formatted into the first column.

> **The Benefits of Exercise**
>
> Whallop! It's hit you!! When your most energetic event over the last few weeks was getting up to change the TV channel because the remote control wasn't working, you suddenly realise that physical exertion can be quite unpleasant!
>
> But fear not! After only a short spell at an activity class the benefits will start to show. You can expect an increase in stamina (those stairs wont seem so steep anymore), strengthening and toning of your once invisible muscles, and an increase in the range of movement of those aching joints.

Save the document as **News1**.

activity 8.2: Charts and Images in Multi-Column Documents.

Charts and images can be imported into multi-column documents in much the same way as they are imported into a single column document. The main differences are:

❑ They may be too big to place in one column and may therefore need sizing or need to occupy two columns.

❑ We may wish to display them across more than one column.

Sizing an Image or a Chart

To size an image or a chart:

❐ Select the chart or image

❐ Drag a sizing handle on the graphic until it is the size that you want.

For more precision you can measure the width of each column and add to that the space between the columns. Select the graphic and use *Format-Picture* to make the total measurement equal to the width of the graphic. You may also need adjust the height of the graphic.

exercise 8.3

We wish to import the image created in session 7 called Stick, into our document **News1**.

❐ Place the insertion point below the existing text.

❐ Open the image file **Stick**. Click on the image and use *Edit-Copy*.

❐ Move back to the window showing **News1** and apply *Edit-Paste* to insert the image into the document.

❐ Size the image by clicking on it to select it and dragging its handles to fit the column. Add a thin line border.

exercise 8.4

Next, at the bottom of the first column we would like to insert the following advertisement:

New Fitness Centre

Fight the Flab
in Chelmer Leisure and Recreation Centre's
New Fitness Suite

Opening 12th September 1993

❐ Move the insertion point below the image and type in the advertisement to fill the first column.

❐ Centre all of the text and format it appropriately.

❐ Apply a border by first selecting the text, and then using *Format-Borders and Shading*.

activity 8.3 Working with hanging indents, tab stops and tables in columns

Hanging indents, tab stops and tables can be used in columns in much the same way as they are used in single column documents. The only problem is likely to be that if you have originally created a table in a single column format and then try to insert it into a two column document, for instance, it will probably be too wide and will need reformatting.

exercise 8.5

In this exercise you will insert the following text into the second column of **News1**, using a hanging indent:

❏ At the top of the second column on the first page enter 'Summer 1993'. In order to get to the top of the second column use **Insert-Break** and choose **Column** to force a column break.

❏ Centre this text, format the text, and place a border around it.

❏ Type in the heading below and centre it.

❏ Press **ENTER** to move onto the next line.

❏ Click on the numbering icon for automatic numbering. Use **Format-Bullets and Numbering** to alter the font of the numbers using **Modify** and **Font**.

❏ Type in the text below:

Six Sun Safe Tips For Sensible Tanning

1. Apply sun cream 30 minutes before going out in the sun and use sun cream all year round.

2. Avoid sun bathing between 11.00am and 3.00pm

3. Reapply sun cream regularly – cream can be removed by swimming, sweating and drying off.

4. Pace yourself! – don't take too much sun too soon. Melanomas take a few days to develop.

5. Keep babies and small children out of strong sun.

6. Always use moisturiser after sun bathing to prevent dry skin and peeling.

❏ Place a border around the text using **Format-Borders and Shading**.

❏ Add the paragraph of text shown at the bottom of the second column of the newsletter.

❏ Save the document as **News1**.

exercise 8.6

In this exercise we insert part of a document that uses tabs into our column.

❑ Insert a column break to place the insertion point at the top of the first column on the second page.

❑ Open the document called **Times**, and select the part of the document relating to both the Health and Fitness Suite opening times.

❑ *Edit-Copy* this selection.

❑ Return to the Window displaying the newsletter, and choose **Edit-*Paste***.

❑ You may need to move the tab stops in order to align the text appropriately. Select the text and experiment with different tab stop positions by dragging them on the ruler, and if necessary different font sizes. You may wish to abbreviate the text slightly. Try to fill the column.

exercise 8.7

In this exercise we introduce a table into a column.

❑ Insert the text shown at the bottom of the first and top of the second column on the second page in the newsletter, entitled: 'Fat, where's it at?'

❑ Choose *Table-Insert Table*. Choose 3 columns.

❑ Enter the text shown in the table on the newsletter into the table, using **TAB** to move between cells.

❑ Apply a border to the table using *Format-Borders and Shading*. Choose an appropriate line and a Grid.

exercise 8.8

In this exercise we add a graph to our newsletter:

❑ First type in the text entitled Step Aerobics.

❑ Now, open the document **Aerobics** created in Exercise 6.10, or quickly create this document. **Aerobics** contains a small pie chart.

❑ Select the pie chart and use *Edit-Copy*.

❑ Return to the Window that displays the newsletter, and use *Edit-Paste*.

❑ The chart should appear in the newsletter.

❏ You may wish to size the chart to make it fit the column, by clicking on it to select it and then pulling its handles.

❏ Save the document as **News1.**

Now perform the formatting for the bottom of page 2.

❏ Choose *View-Header and Footer.*

❏ Click on **Page Setup** button in the **Header and Footer** toolbar. Under the Layout 'tab' check the **Different First Page** box. Click on **OK**

❏ Switch to the footer and click on the **Show Next** button. Type in the following text:

'For bookings and details of any activities and classes at Chelmer Leisure and Recreation Centre Please Ring: 091-336-6612.'

❏ Format the text to a size that makes it legible

❏ Place a border around the text, using *Format-Borders and Shading*.

❏ Click on the **Close** button.

When you have completed Exercise 8.8 you should have created the newsletter shown on the next two pages.

integrative exercises

exercise 8.9

This exercise asks you to create the text that follows the newsletter as one side of a leaflet or flyer.

The text uses three columns and some text formatting. This exercise should be much simpler than the exercise that you may just have completed on the newsletter. Here are the basic steps:

❏ Open a new document.

❏ Choose *File-Page Setup* and alter the page orientation to landscape.

❏ Choose *Format-Columns* and select three columns to **Apply** to the **Whole Document**.

❏ Enter the text in the first column. Apply borders, centring and character formatting as appropriate.

❏ Continue to type in the text for the next two columns formatting it as appropriate.

Chelmer Leisure and Recreation Centre

Fitness and Health Suites

Fully air conditioned

Satellite TV

Computerised video screen

Cardio-vascular equipment

Fitness testing

Super circuit training

Sauna and steam rooms

Jacuzzi relaxation lounge

Sunbeds

Personalised diets

Beauty therapy

A unique combination of superb facilities

The Health and Fitness Suites represent a superb facility.

Fitness Suite

The fitness suite is for all sizes, ages and fitness levels. It offers an environment where care and attention to users' needs are of paramount importance.

Each person is carefully assessed and taught how to use the equipment to maximise their potential. Don't worry about your level of fitness – our staff are on hand to help and advise you on how to progress enjoyably and safely.

Super Circuit Training. For the energetic, special Super Circuit training sessions are available.

Personalised Exercise Programmes and Fitness Testing Option. Personalised exercise programmes are available with an added option of a fitness test.

Fitness testing has become an important ingredient in the recipe for improved fitness. It tells you your current fitness

level and provides a tailor made programme with personal fitness targets.

Health Suite

Our superb health suite offers all of the facilities necessary to relax, unwind and let the day's worries drift away. These include:

Sauna & Steam Room. Relax in either the Sauna or Steam Room. Ideal after a hard workout, long day or simply for pure relaxation.

Power Shower. Whether you like your showers hot or cold foam, spray or jet, we have just the shower to suit your needs.

Jacuzzi Relaxation Lounge with Satellite TV. Immerse yourself in jets of warm water and gently soothing bubbles whi;e you unwind and alleviate stress from work and everyday life.

Sunbeds. Our three new Ultrabronze tanning beds use the latest RUVA tubes and also offer high pressure facial panels.

exercise 8.10

This exercise asks you to create a front page which uses columns for part of the page.

❏ Open the document **Front** that you created in Exercise 2.11.

❏ Choose **View-Page Layout**

❏ Remove all borders. (Word will not apply continuous borders across sections).

❏ Place the insertion point below the centred text.

❏ We wish to reposition the students and tutors name to display it as indicated below. Select the text at the bottom of the page.

❏ Choose **Format-Columns**, and select two columns and **Apply To: Selected Text**.

❏ Place the pointer at the end of the tutors name and insert a column break with **Insert-Column Break** and then **OK**.

❏ Now select the text in the first column and apply left alignment.

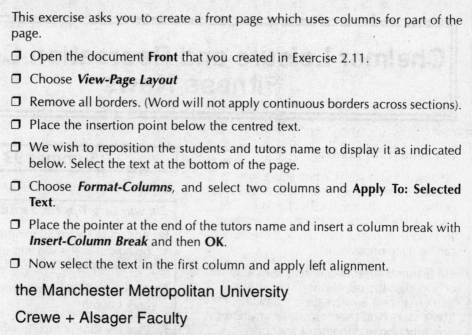

the Manchester Metropolitan University

Crewe + Alsager Faculty

Environment & Enterprise Project

The Refurbishment of the Multi-Gym into a Fitness Suite at Chelmer Leisure and Recreation Centre

A Feasibility Study

By: Sarah Leveridge
Tutor: R. S. Symmond

Course: HND Business and Finance
Date: 1st February 1995

Chelmer Leisure and Recreation Centre Fitness News

The Benefits of Exercise

Whallop! It's hit you!! When your most energetic event over the last few weeks was getting up to change the TV channel because the remote control wasn't working, you suddenly realise that physical exertion can be quite unpleasant!

But fear not! After only a short spell at an activity class the benefits will start to show. You can expect an increase in stamina (those stairs won't seem so steep anymore), strengthening and toning of your once invisible muscles, and an increase in the range of movement of those aching joints.

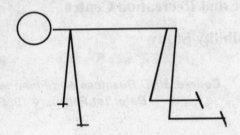

New Fitness Centre

Fight the Flab

in Chelmer Leisure and Recreation Centre's
New Fitness Suite

Opening 12th September 1993

Summer 93

Six Sun Safe Tips For Sensible Tanning

1. Apply sun cream 30 minutes before going out in the sun and use sun cream all year round.

2. Avoid sun bathing between 11.00am and 3.00pm

3. Reapply sun cream regularly - cream can be removed by swimming, sweating and drying off.

4. Pace yourself! - don't take too much sun too soon. Melanomas take a few days to develop.

5. Keep babies and small children out of strong sun.

6. Always use moisturiser after sun bathing to prevent dry skin and peeling.

The month is May, the sun may shine and the melanomas may not be too far behind. The need for creaming up has never been greater!

The strength of your cream is governed by its SPF - Sun Protection Factor. This gives you an indication as to how long you can stay in the sun without melting. The higher the SPF the greater the protection provided. The choice of an appropriate SPF depends upon your skin type and how it usually reacts to the sun.

Opening Times

Health Suite

Monday	9.00am - 9.00pm	Ladies Only
Tuesday	9.00am - 9.00pm	Mixed
Wednesday	9.30am - 9.00pm	Mixed
Thursday	9.00am - 1.00pm	Ladies Only
	1.00pm - 9.00pm	Mixed
Friday	9.00am - 9.00pm	Men Only
Saturday	9.00am - 1.00pm	Men Only
	1.00pm - 5.00pm	Mixed
Sunday	9.00am - 5.00pm	Mixed

Fitness Suite

Monday	8.00am - 8.00pm	
	8.00pm - 9.00pm	Super Circuit
Tuesday	9.00am - 9.00pm	
Wednesday	9.30am - 8.00pm	
	8.00pm - 9.00pm	Super Circuit
Thursday	9.00am - 9.00pm	
Friday	9.00am - 9.00pm	
Saturday	9.00am - 5.00pm	
Sunday	9.00am - 5.00pm	

Fat, where's it at?

Fat plays an important part in all of our lives. It is widely accepted that reducing fat from our diet is a positive move but does that mean all fat?

Saturated fats, the most unhealthy, are fats which are solid at room temperature. Examples include animal fats and brazil nuts. Mono-unsaturated fats can either be solid or liquid at room temperature and these include vegetable fats and olive oil. Fats which are soft or liquid at room

temperature are polyunsaturated. These can be found in fish oils and vegetable oils.

A fatty diet can result in obesity with many of its attendant health risks: high blood pressure, diabetes, gall bladder disease, arthritis, surgical risks and coronary heart disease, to name but a few. The table below shows the recommended limits on fats for the average *quite active* person.

	Saturated Fat	Other Fats
80Kg Man	35g	82g
61Kg Woman	27g	63g

Step Aerobics

The chart below shows how popular Step Aerobics has become. Have you tried step aerobics? It is a popular means of getting and keeping fit.

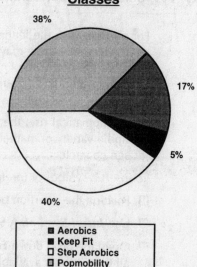

Popularity of Exercise Classes

38%

17%

5%

40%

- ■ Aerobics
- ■ Keep Fit
- ☐ Step Aerobics
- ▨ Popmobility

For bookings and details of any activities and classes at Chelmer Leisure and Recreation Centre please ring:

0191-336 6612

Session 9
Special applications

objectives

This session collects together a number of special applications. After this session you should be able to create documents containing:

❐ Foreign words

❐ simple mathematical and scientific formulae

❐ more complex formulae using the equation editor

Other slightly more advanced techniques that can be used in document creation will be examined, these being

❐ performing calculations

❐ using fields

❐ interfacing with other software

❐ mail merge

activity 9.1 Scientific, mathematical and foreign symbols

For normal work the letters and symbols that appear on the keyboard are sufficient. However, there may be occasions where a foreign word containing symbols that are not in the English alphabet needs to be included. Another area in which non-standard letters are required is in the production of a scientific or mathematical document.

For mathematical use, the Windows Symbol typefont contains the Greek alphabet and a variety of mathematical symbols. In the typefont Normal Text there are foreign characters.

To insert a symbol or foreign letter:

❐ Position the insertion point where the character is to appear.

❐ Use *Insert-Symbol*. A **Symbol** dialog box appears.

❐ Open the drop down **Font** list box and select the particular font required and all the symbols available in that font will be displayed in a grid.

❐ A symbol is selected using the pointer by pointing and clicking, the chosen symbol is displayed in a larger size as white text on a blue background (default colours).

❐ To insert the symbol into the document click on **Insert**. The symbol will take the current point size that is being used.

exercise 9.1

Start a new document, selecting symbols from (normal text) and Symbol, key in the following:

fête   café Σx $a \geq b$ 100°C

Defining Foreign Language Portions of a Document

If a portion of a document, or indeed all of it, is to be written in a foreign language then Word needs to be made aware of this. You will not want Word to spell check a paragraph in, say, French using an English dictionary. If French proofing tools (spelling and grammar) are available these are used instead.

To format text as being in a foreign language:

❒ Select the text.

❒ Choose **Tools-Language** and in the dialog box select the language required. Click on **OK.**

activity 9.2 The equation editor

One of the most difficult tasks in word processing is to write an equation, particularly if the equation has a complicated structure. Lining up numerator and denominator, positioning brackets, using sub and superscripts, to name but a few, are typical of the problems encountered when constructing an equation. Word provides a means to overcome this in the form of an equation editor. The equation editor will not be examined in detail, however the basics will be covered.

The equation editor works in the same way as Graph, i.e. a separate window runs the editor program, in which the equation is constructed and when finished *File-Exit and Return to document* is used to embed the equation into the document. As with graph the equation may be edited by double-clicking on it to return to the editor program.

Starting the Equation Editor

The equation editor is available through the **Insert-Object** command. An object dialog box appears and the first option highlighted is **Equation** (if it is not the first option then click on it to select it). Click on **OK** to select this option. Notice that other 'objects' can be activated through this dialog box.

The equation editor window should appear and as for Graph it is advisable to maximise it to prevent accidental clicking on the document window behind. Maximising also provides more room in which to work.

The Editor window

This has standard windows features and also two palette bars below the menu bar. Directly below the menu bar are the symbol palettes and below that are the template palettes. The insertion point looks different, it is flashing vertical and horizontal lines inside a dotted rectangle known as a slot.

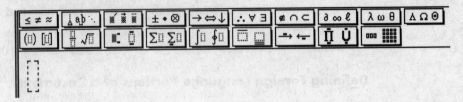

Building an equation

It is best to write down the equation to be created so that its method of construction can be considered. The basic rule for creating an equation is set up template first and then fill the slots in the template with symbols. An equation template is the layout of the equation without any symbols. The following exercise demonstrates how to build an equation by selecting templates and then filling them with symbols. If the wrong template is inserted by mistake use **Edit-Undo** to remove it.

Templates are chosen from the lower palette bar. The icons in this bar represent the categories of template. By clicking and holding the mouse button on one of these icons a sub-menu appears showing all the templates available in that category. Still holding the mouse button down move to the one required and release the button. Symbols can be inserted into the template to complete the equation.

It is beyond the scope of this session to go into very much detail concerning equation creation. However, by illustrating the creation some basic statistical equations encountered by business students, it is hoped to provide a firm base from which to explore the capabilities of the equation editor.

exercise 9.2

The equation to be produced is that for calculating the mean value of a set of grouped data.

$$\bar{x} = \frac{\sum fx_{mid}}{\sum f}$$

Start a new document:

❐ Position the insertion point at the place where the equation is to be and use **Insert-Object Equation**.

❐ Type **x**. Select the third icon on the **symbols** bar. Click and hold. Move to the first box in the fourth row. Release.

❐ Type =. It is worth noting at this point that you cannot type a space into an equation, the editor sorts out the spacing.

❐ Select the second icon on the **template** bar. Click and hold. Move to the first box in the first row. Release.

- ❒ Select the fourth icon on the **template** bar. Click and hold. Move to the first box in the first row. Release.
- ❒ Type **fx**.
- ❒ Select the third icon on the **template** bar. Click and hold. Move to the second box in the first row. Release.
- ❒ Type **mid**.
- ❒ Press ↓ to move to the denominator part of the equation.
- ❒ Using a template insert a as for the numerator.
- ❒ Type **f**. Use ***File-Exit and Return to Document.*** Answer **Yes** to save changes to equation in document.

exercise 9.3

Keeping open the document just created, save it as **Stats**. On a new line create the following equation for the standard deviation of ungrouped data:

$$\sigma' = \sqrt{\frac{\sum (x - \bar{x})^2}{n}}$$

- ❒ Position the insertion point at the place where the equation is to be and use ***Insert-Object Equation***.
- ❒ Select the ninth icon on the **symbols** bar. Click and hold. Move to the letter which is first on the sixth row. Release. Type **=**.
- ❒ Select the second icon on the **template** bar. Click and hold. Move to the first box in the fourth row. Release.
- ❒ Select the second icon on the **template** bar. Click and hold. Move to the first box in the first row. Release.
- ❒ Select the fourth icon on the **template** bar. Click and hold. Move to the first box in the first row. Release.
- ❒ Select the first icon on the **template** bar. Click and hold. Move to the first box in the first row. Release.
- ❒ Type **x-x**.
- ❒ Select the third icon on the **symbols** bar. Click and hold. Move to the first box in the fourth row. Release.
- ❒ Press → to move to the insertion point to the end of the brackets.
- ❒ Select the third icon on the **template** bar. Click and hold. Move to the first box in the first row. Release. Type **2**.
- ❒ Press ↓ four times to move to the denominator slot. Make sure the insertion point is flashing in this slot.
- ❒ Type **n**. Use ***File-Exit and Return to Document.*** Answer **Yes** to save changes. Save the document.

exercise 9.4

Finally add the equation to find the gradient of a line of best fit.

$$m = \frac{\sum xy - \dfrac{\sum x \sum y}{n}}{\sum x^2 - \dfrac{\left(\sum x\right)^2}{n}}$$

- ❏ Position the insertion point at the place where the equation is to be and use *Insert-Object Equation*.
- ❏ Type **m=**. Select the second icon on the **template** bar. Click and hold. Move to the first box in the first row. Release.
- ❏ Select the fourth icon on the **template** bar. Click and hold. Move to the first box in the first row. Release. Type **xy-**.
- ❏ Select the second icon on the **template** bar. Click and hold. Move to the first box in the first row. Release.
- ❏ Select the fourth icon on the **template** bar. Click and hold. Move to the first box in the first row. Release. Type **x.**
- ❏ Select the fourth icon on the **template** bar. Click and hold. Move to the first box in the first row. Release. Type **y.**
- ❏ Press ↓ and type **n**.
- ❏ Click in the denominator slot to move the insertion point.
- ❏ Select the fourth icon on the **template** bar. Click and hold. Move to the first box in the first row. Release. Type **x.**
- ❏ Select the third icon on the **template** bar. Click and hold. Move to the first box in the first row. Release. Type **2**.
- ❏ Press ↓ and type **-**.
- ❏ Select the second icon on the **template** bar. Click and hold. Move to the first box in the first row. Release.
- ❏ Select the first icon on the **template** bar. Click and hold. Move to the first box in the first row. Release.
- ❏ Select the fourth icon on the **template** bar. Click and hold. Move to the first box in the first row. Release. Type **x** and press → twice to move the insertion point to the end of the brackets.
- ❏ Select the third icon on the **template** bar. Click and hold. Move to the first box in the first row. Release. Type **2**.
- ❏ Click in the denominator slot.
- ❏ Type **n**. Use *File-Exit and Return to Document.* Answer **Yes** to save changes to equation in document.

Adjusting settings in the Equation Editor

To make adjustments to the font and size of an equation use either *Format-Style* or *Size-Define*. *Format-Style* will allow different type fonts to be applied and *Size-Define* will allow the size of the individual parts that make up an equation to be altered.

activity 9.3 Calculations

Basic mathematical calculations can be performed within a Word document. Word allows figures to be added, subtracted, multiplied, and divided. Word assumes that you will perform calculations in a table, in a manner similar to using a spreadsheet. It also offers some spreadsheet formatting and functions, such as MAX, MIN, and AVERAGE. The *Formula* command which is only available on the *Table* menu is the method Word uses to perform calculations.

Adding figures in a table

Often figures are that presented in a tabular form are totalled and the *Table-Formula* command can be used. The exercise below illustrates this process.

exercise 9.5

Into a new document, key in the following table:

Adult	140
Junior	20
Concessionary	70
Club Adult	20
Club Junior	10
Total	

❏ Position the insertion point in the cell in the table where the answer is to appear, i.e. the empty cell opposite Total.

❏ Choose *Table-Formula*. A **Formula** dialog box appears in which Word proposes a formula, in this case =SUM(ABOVE), which means it will total the column above the cell selected. Click on **OK** and the answer, 260, will be inserted into the table.

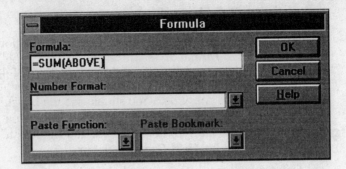

exercise 9.6

Start a new document. Enter the following table with which some simple formulas will be used.

3	4	
3	4	

❑ Position the insertion point in the empty cell at the top of the third column.

❑ Choose **Table-Formula**. A **Formula** dialog box appears in which the proposed formula is =SUM(LEFT), which means it will total the row to the left of the cell selected. Click on **OK** and the answer, 7, will be inserted into the table.

❑ Imagine that the each column in the table is denoted by a letter of the alphabet (so in the table above there are columns A, B, and C) and that each row in the table is denoted by a number (rows 1, 2, and 3). Each cell in the table can be uniquely identified by its 'grid reference', i.e. the top left cell is A1 and the bottom right cell is C3. If you have used a spreadsheet you will be familiar with this concept.

❑ Position the insertion point in cell C2. Use **Table-Formula** and edit the proposed formula so that it reads =A2*B2 instead. Click on **OK**. The * means multiply, is the answer what you expected?

❑ Position the insertion point in cell A3. Use **Table-Formula** and edit the proposed formula so that it reads =C2/A1 instead. Click on **OK**. The / means divide.

❑ Position the insertion point in cell B3. Use **Table-Formula** and edit the proposed formula so that it reads =C2-C1 instead. Click on **OK**. The – means subtract.

❑ Position the insertion point in cell C3. Use **Table-Formula** and edit the proposed formula so that it reads =SUM(A1:C2) instead. Click on **OK**. What has been calculated?

activity 9.4 Using Fields

Fields are instructions to Word to perform a certain task. You will probably have inserted fields into a document without realising it. Recall the file Fattips from exercise 2.9 and use *Tools-Options,* select the **View** 'tab' and under Show check the **Field Code** check box. You should see the bullets change into some strange text enclosed in curly brackets, this is an instruction to Word to use the bullet character. Use *Tools-Options* again to change back to the usual view by removing the x from the **Field Code** check box.

Fields can be quite complicated and it is not the intention to go into very much detail on this subject. Therefore only two types of fields which might be used in the type of work produced by a reader will be considered. These are the date field and sequence numbering fields. Having a flavour for these may encourage the more serious user to experiment with other field types.

The date field

This is useful particularly in a standard letter or memo template.

exercise 9.7

This exercise will insert a date field into the file **Appmemo**. Open the file **Appmemo** created in exercise 2.3. Following the instructions

❏ Position the insertion point at the place where the date is to go.

❏ Choose *Insert-Date and Time.*

❏ Select the format of the date from the **Date and Time** box. Click **OK**.

Updating the date

The date field will not automatically update so that if you were to open the memo, created in the last exercise, in a few days time the date would still be that of when the field was created.

To update the field:

❏ Select the date.

❏ Press **F9**.

Using Fields to Sequence Numbers

This field type is useful if you have a numbering sequence for, chapters, sections, paragraphs, figures, tables etc. in your document. It saves having to check back through the document to see what the last number in the sequence was. To insert a sequence field:

❏ Position the insertion point at the place in the document where the number is to go.

Either

☐ Choose *Insert-Field* select **Numbering** from **Categories** and **Seq** from **Field Names**.

☐ Click in the **Field Code** box after **seq** and type the name of the sequence of numbers e.g. table for a sequence of numbers for tables. Click **OK.**

or

☐ Press **CTRL+F9** and inside the curly brackets (which are not ordinary curly brackets) type **seq table.**

☐ Press **F9.**

This kind of field code may be viewed individually by positioning the insertion point in the field, clicking the right mouse button and selecting **Toggle field code**.

Note that care must be taken to ensure that the fields are updated. For example, a table might be added or removed from the document. Fields may be updated individually as described for the date field or in the case of a sequence the whole document can be selected and all fields will be updated by pressing **F9**.

exercise 9.8

For this exercise create a document containing some tables from session 4.

☐ Open a new document.

☐ Using *Insert-File* insert the following documents into the new document, **Times, Fatlim, Address,** and **Timetble.**

☐ Leave a line space between each table.

☐ Below each table

   1.   type Table;

   2.   press CTRL+F9 and shaded curly brackets appear;

   3.   in between the curly brackets type seq table;

   4.   press F9 to turn the field into a number.

☐ Save the document as **Tables.**

activity 9.5 Interfacing with other software

Word interfaces well with other Windows applications, particularly those written by Microsoft. It will also interface will other software.

Importing text files

It is possible to import text which has been directly created by another word processor or by the previous versions of Word. When *File-Open* is used if *.* is typed into the **File Name** box then all files in the directory are listed. Many word processors produce documents files with the extension .doc but text files may have other extensions such as .txt or .exp.

If a file is selected that was not created by Word a further dialog box appears with a list of **Files of Type**. Word will highlight the type of file which it believes the file is of. Either accept Word's choice or select the type of file required and click on **OK**.

Exporting files for use with other software

To do this use *File-Save As* and open the **Save File as Type** list box. Select the type of format required and save as normal. For example the document can be saved in a WordPerfect for Windows format.

Interfacing with other windows applications

Within windows the clipboard can be used to import text or graphics from other windows applications. The ability to interface with Excel has already been mentioned. Graphics, for example, from the Windows Paintbrush application can be imported via the clipboard.

activity 9.6 Mail Merge

The word 'mailshot' is commonly used in the business environment. It means to send out many duplicated letters to a target audience, often for advertising or market research. A word processor's mail merge facility can 'personalise' a standard letter so that for example the recipient's name and address are printed. The following exercise describes using Word to perform a simple mail merge.

exercise 9.9

Two documents are required for a mail merge

1. The **standard letter**. This contains the standard text plus areas which are marked as 'replaceable' i.e. personal information can be slotted into them.

2. The **data document**. This is a document containing the personal information which is to be slotted into the standard letter. Each person's information is in a separate paragraph.

Note: an existing table, such as the one created in exercise 4.6, can be used as a data document in a mail merge. Data in each row of the table is 'slotted into' the standard letter, i.e. one letter per row.

First make a plan of the standard letter to decide which information is to be replaceable. In this example the replaceable information is name, company, street, town, county and postcode. If you browse forwards you will see the layout of the letter. It is simplest to create both of these documents in the same directory. Word will help you through three stages of mail merging. The first stage is to create the standard letter (the main document).

☐ Open a new document.

☐ Key in the address of the centre, using a date field for the current date, as follows:

Chelmer Leisure and Recreation Centre
Park View Road
Chelmer
Cheshire
CE9 5JS

12th October 1993

☐ Save the document as **Mail**.

☐ Choose *Tools-Mail Merge* and the following dialog box appears:

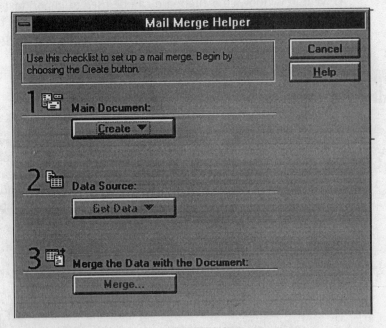

☐ Click on the **Create** button. Choose **Form Letter** and click on the **Active Window** button. The next step is to specify the data source or to create the data source.

☐ Choose **Create Data Source** and the **Create Data Source** dialog box is displayed. In this box you define the names of your replaceable fields.

☐ Click on **FirstName** (in the Field Names in Header Row box) and click on the **Remove Field Name** button. Repeat for all fields except Title, LastName, Company, and PostalCode.

☐ Type Street into the **Field Name** box and check on **Add Field Name**. Repeat for Town and again for County. Use the 'Move' arrow buttons to reorder the field headers so that they are in the order Title, LastName, Company, Street, Town, County, and PostalCode.

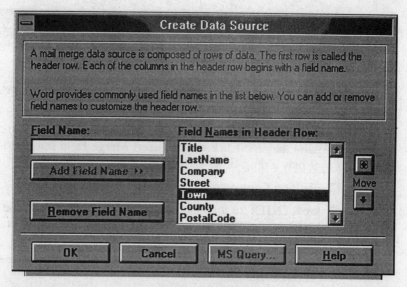

- Click on **OK**. Save your data source as **Supplier**.

- Choose **Edit Data Source** and a form for entering data records will be displayed.

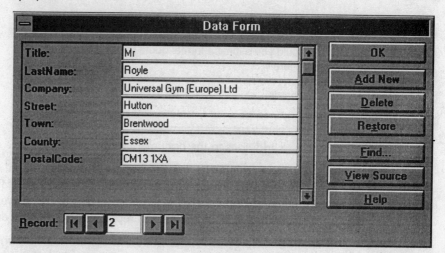

- Enter the following records. Hint: use the TAB key to move from one box to the next. After each record is entered click on the **Add New** button, until the last one is complete and then click on **OK**.

Title	LastName	Company	Street	Town	County	PostalCode
Mrs	Allen	Medlock Leisure Centre	Fold Avenue	Droylsen	Tameside	DR17 5TG
Mr	Royle	Universal Gym (Europe) Ltd	Hutton	Brentwood	Essex	CM13 1XA
Mr	Bradbury	Atlanta Sports Industries Ltd	Atlanta House	Maltby	Rotherham	S66 8QN
Miss	Jackson	Physique Training Equipment Ltd	Bankfield Mill	Colne	Lancashire	BB8 9PD

- Save this as **Supplier.** You will return to the letter document. Notice that there is an extra toolbar for mail merging.

☐ If you wish to edit your data file click on the **Mail Merge Helper** button otherwise carry on to the next step.

☐ Position the insertion point for the first line of the company address. Click on the **Insert Merge Field** button to display a drop-down list of the fields in the data file.

☐ Click on **Company.**

☐ Press **ENTER** for the next line of the address, click on the **Insert Merge Field** button and highlight **Street.** Build up the address and greeting as shown below:

```
<<Company>>
<<Street>>
<<Town>>
<<County>>
<<PostalCode>>

Dear <<Title>> <<LastName>>
Thank you for your interest in providing equipment for our new fitness suite.
Please could you submit a formal quote for our consideration.
Yours sincerely

G. V. Richards
Manager
```

☐ Save these additions to the document **Mail.**

 ☐ You may wish to click on the tick button in the merge tool bar to check the data file. The most common error is where the number of fields in a record does not correspond with the number of fields that have been specified. Choose the Simulate the merge and report errors in a new document option.

 ☐ Click on the **Merge to Printer** button in the tool bar to print the merged letters. One letter will be produced for each record of data.

☐ If you wish to merge the letters to a file rather than printing them, this can be done by clicking on the **Merge to New Document** on the tool bar. Each letter in the new document will be separated from the next by a section break. Don't forget to save this new document if you wish to keep the merge for later printing.

Appendix 1
Basic Windows Operations

Some readers will not be familiar with Windows and Word may well be one of the first Windows products encountered by many users. Any reader who has not previously used Windows is strongly recommended to run through the Windows tutorial which introduces users to mouse techniques and the basic operation of Windows. This appendix briefly summarises some of the key operations and should act as a ready reference to some of the terminology that is used elsewhere in the book.

Mouse Techniques

The basic mouse techniques are listed in the table below, with a simple description of each technique.

To	Do This
Point	Position the mouse pointer on or next to something
Click	Position the pointer and then quickly press and release the left mouse button
Double click	Position the pointer and then quickly press and release the left mouse button twice
Drag	Position the pointer. Press and hold down the left mouse button as you move the mouse to the desired position. The release the button.

Mouse Pointer Shapes

When the mouse is pointed to different parts of the screen, the pointer shape changes allowing you to perform different tasks. Some commands also change the pointer shape.

If the pointer assumes a shape that you do not want to use, press ESC to restore the pointer to its usual shape.

The table below lists some common pointer shapes as encountered in Word:

Pointer shape	Meaning
I	The pointer in the text area. This pointer indicates where to begin typing

↕ ↔   These pointers appear in print preview when the pointer is over the margin bars at the top or left of the screen.

↖   The pointer is in the menus, inactive windows scroll bars, ribbon, ruler or Toolbar. You can choose a menu and command, click a button, or drag a tab stop marker. thisis also the sizing arrow when you have a picture selected. You may drag the sizing handles to scale or crop the picture.

↗   The pointer is in the selection bar (at left edge of screen), the style name bar along the window's left edge or in table selection bars. You can select a line, paragraph, or the entire document.

⧗   Word is performing a task that will take a few seconds

↖?   The pointer appears after you press the Help key. You can point to any item on the screen and click to view specific Help.

↕   This pointer appears when the mouse pointer is on the split box in the vertical scroll bar.

↔| The pointer is on the style name area (see Appendix 3) split line. Drag to change the width of the style name area.

↕   The pointer is on a window border, and you can change the vertical size of a window.

↔   You can change the horizontal size of a window

↘   You can change the diagonal size of a window.

✛   This pointer appears when you have selected the Move or Size command from the Control menu. You can move the window to a new position or drag the window border.

✛   This pointer appears in Outline View, when positioned on a selection symbol. It indicates that you can drag the heading or frame.

↔   This pointer appears in Outline View as you drag a heading left or right to a new level in the outline. It also appears when positioned over a frame handle, indicating that you can size the frame by dragging the handle.

↕   This pointer appears in Outline View as you drag a heading up or down to a new position. It also appears when positioned over a frame handle, indicating that you can size the frame by dragging the handle.

↓ The pointer is over a column in a table. Click to select the column.

This pointer appears when you select text or a graphic and press a mouse button to drag the selection to its new location, where you drop or insert it.

This is the format painter pointer which can be used to select parts of a document to which a certain selection is to be applied.

Basics of Windows: A Quick Review

The following are the elements of a basic Windows screen.

Menu Bar

The menu bar shows the titles of the various pull down menus that are available with a given application. To select a menu option, first select the menu by placing the mouse pointer over the name of the menu on the menu bar and click the left mouse button. The menu will appear. Move the mouse pointer to the menu option you require and click the left mouse button again. Note that any menu options displayed in light grey are not currently available. Menus can also be accessed via the keyboard. For example, to select the file menu press **ALT+F** i.e. press **ALT** together with the initial letter of the menu option.

Control Menu

The control menu is found on all windows whether they be application windows or document windows. To access the Control menu click on the control menu box in the upper left corner of the window, or press **ALT+SPACEBAR**. The exact contents are different for different windows, but typically basic windows operations such as restore, move, size, minimise, maximise, close and switch to are represented.

Title Bar

The title bar tells you which window is displayed. By pointing the mouse at the window's title bar , and then dragging the title bar to a new location the window can removed.

Maximise, Minimise and Restore Buttons

Clicking on the **MAXIMISE** button enlarges a window to its maximum size, so that is fills the whole desktop.

Clicking on the **RESTORE** button will restore a maximised window to its previous size.

Clicking on the **MINIMISE** button reduces the window to a small icon at the bottom of the screen. When you shrink an application window to an icon, the application is still running in memory, but its window is not taking up space on your desktop.

Dialog Boxes

Windows uses dialog boxes to request information from you and to provide information to you. Most dialog boxes include options, with each option asking for a different kind of information.

After all of the requested information has been supplied you choose a command button to carry out the command. Two command buttons that feature on every dialog box are OK and CANCEL. OK causes the command to be executed. CANCEL cancels the operation and removes the dialog box from the screen. These buttons represent the two means of quitting from a dialog box. To choose a command button, click on it, or if the button is currently active, press ENTER.

There are a number of different kinds of controls in dialog boxes. These are:

Text boxes are boxes where you are allowed to type in text, such as a filename. The presence of a flashing vertical bar, or the insertion point, indicates that the text box is active and that you may enter text. If the text box is not active, place the mouse pointer on the box and click. The insertion point will then appear in the box.

List boxes show a column of available choices. Items can be selected from a list box by double clicking on the item, or clicking once on the item and then clicking on the OK button.

Check boxes offer a list of options that you can switch on and off. You can select as many or as few check box options as are applicable. When an option in a check box is selected it contains an X; otherwise the box is empty. To select a check box, click on the empty box.

Option buttons appear as a list of mutually exclusive items. You can select only one option from the list at a time. You can change a selection by selecting a different button. The selected button contains a black dot. To select an option button, click on it.

Scroll bars appear at the side of windows and list boxes. They appear when the information contained in a window can not be displayed wholly within that window. Both vertical and horizontal scroll bars may be present depending on whether the document is too long or too wide to fit on the screen. The small box in the middle of the bar represents the position of the currently displayed text within the whole document. You can move to a different position in the text by moving this box. You can move this box either by clicking on the scroll bar arrow boxes, clicking on the scroll bar itself, or dragging the box.

Buttons on the standard and formatting toolbars

The following table lists the default buttons that appear on the standard and formatting toolbars, and shows their functions.

Standard Toolbar

	New	Opens a new document based on current default setting
	Open	Opens an existing document or template. The Open dialog box is displayed so that you can locate and open a specified file
	Save	Saves the active dcument or template with its current name. If the document has not been named the **Save As** dialog box will be displayed
	Print	Prints all pages of the active document
	Print Preview	Previews the active document
	Spelling	Check the spelling of the document or selected sections
	Cut	Removes selected text and graphics and stores them on the clipboard
	Copy	Copies selected text and graphics and stores them on the clipboard
	Paste	Inserts the contents of thw clipboard at the insertion point or selection
	Format Painter	Once you've formatted text to look the way you want you can copy this formatting to other selected text. Click once on this button to copy one selection, double-click to copy several
	Undo	Reverses the action that you last performed
	Redo	Reverses the action of undo
	AutoFormat	Automatically formats the text by applying styles from the attached template
	Edit AutoText	Use to quickly create or insert an AutoText entry
	Insert Rows	Inserts rows into a table
	Insert Microsoft Excel Worksheet	Inserts a spreadsheet into the document
	Text columns	Formats the current section of our document with one or multiple newspaper style columns. To select the number of columns, drag over the sample columns that are displayed
	Draw	Displays the Drawing toolbar
	Graph	Starts the Graph program
	Show Hide ¶	Shows or hides the non-printing (white space) characters
	Zoom Control	Open the drop down list to select the zoom percentage
	Help	Click on this button to display the Help pointer

Formatting Toolbar

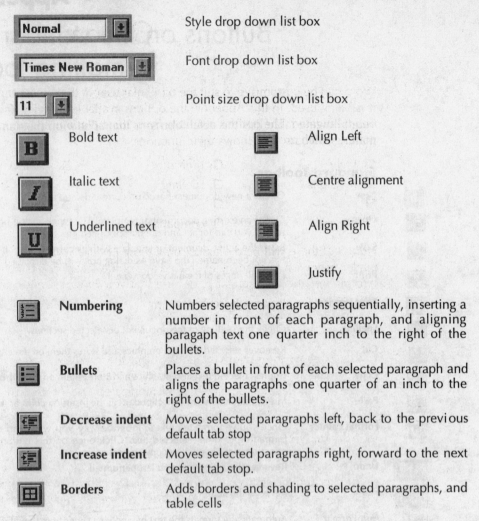

Normal ▼ — Style drop down list box

Times New Roman ▼ — Font drop down list box

11 ▼ — Point size drop down list box

B Bold text

I Italic text

U Underlined text

Align Left

Centre alignment

Align Right

Justify

Numbering — Numbers selected paragraphs sequentially, inserting a number in front of each paragraph, and aligning paragaph text one quarter inch to the right of the bullets.

Bullets — Places a bullet in front of each selected paragraph and aligns the paragraphs one quarter of an inch to the right of the bullets.

Decrease indent — Moves selected paragraphs left, back to the previous default tab stop

Increase indent — Moves selected paragraphs right, forward to the next default tab stop.

Borders — Adds borders and shading to selected paragraphs, and table cells

Appendix 3
Customising Word

Word can be customised to suit the particular user or the circumstances in which it is being used. In this Appendix the options available from the *Tools* menu will be investigated. The options available from *Tools-Options* are grouped into categories, which are:

❑ view	❑ user info	❑ grammar
❑ revisions	❑ spelling	❑ print
❑ save	❑ edit	❑ file locations
❑ general	❑ compatibility	❑ auto format

Not all of these will be discussed, only those options which it is considered the reader may wish to change. To change any of the other options consult the Help information and the manual to be sure that you know the effect of any change you make.

View

In this category the options available affect the window display, text and non-printing characters. You may set the width of the style area which is an area displayed to the left of the document which indicates the style applied to each paragraph.

Windows Display

By clicking in the appropriate check boxes select whether or not to display the scroll bars and the status bar. If the **Style Area** width is increased from its default value of zero, the document is displayed with a left margin showing the style name applied to the corresponding text.

Show and Non-Printing Characters

It is best to leave these options as their default values. There may be occasions when hidden characters such as paragraph marks are required to be seen. However, this is unlikely as it is easy to switch between displaying punctuation marks or not.

Save

Here it is possible to choose between fast saving or creating a backup of your document. It is better to choose to create a backup copy. You may also wish to add or remove the **Summary Information** dialog box which can be used to record summary information about a document. You should get into the habit of saving your work every few minutes or so. If you find this hard Word can do it for you if you set a time in the automatic saving box.

General

Here you can alter the measurement units that Word uses. You may choose between centimetres, inches, points, or picas.

Spelling

Options may be set to allow the spell checker to ignore words that are in upper-case and/or words that contain numbers. Through the **Custom Dictionaries** box it is possible to set up your own dictionary. The **Always Suggest** box may be used to speed up checking if this is off. Also you may select to check spelling from the main dictionary only.

Edit

The one setting you may wish to alter is that of **Typing Replaces Selection** particularly if you are new to Word. New users of Word can make selections by mistake and if this is followed by, say, pressing **ENTER** then the selection disappears. It has been replaced by a paragraph mark. *Edit-Undo* will remedy this but a new user might not recognise what has happened soon enough. If this option is switched off, by clicking in the check box to remove the cross, then this problem is avoided.

Other settings in this category which you may wish to alter are the operation of the drag and drop feature or the selection of text in units of whole words.

Print

There is one option in this section you may wish to use, which is **Reverse Print Order**. This will cause a document to be printed from the last page to the first.

Index

Promoting Active Learning
software guides
for student-centred learning

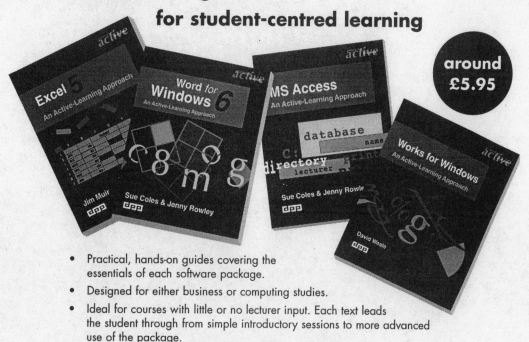

around
£5.95

- Practical, hands-on guides covering the essentials of each software package.

- Designed for either business or computing studies.

- Ideal for courses with little or no lecturer input. Each text leads the student through from simple introductory sessions to more advanced use of the package.

- Realistic business examples give students a relevant context for the features and techniques of the package.

- Free lecturers' disks available for most of the guides for demonstration/checking of students' work.

- '[MS Access is] excellent! Affordable enough for students to buy even for a short course.' Lecturer